Self-Esteem
The Key to Success

Three Electives That Change
the Lives of Kids

People have two basic needs: to know they
are lovable and to know they are worthwhile

By Gail Cassidy

This book is dedicated to the many students I have taught
over the years, especially my VoTech students who
taught me more than I ever taught them.

WHO SHOULD READ THIS BOOK?

ALL EDUCATORS: Teachers, Principals, Superintendents!

WHY READ THIS BOOK?

This book sets out to answer these two questions, "How can an educator best equip a child to succeed and be happy in today's society?" "How can a teacher instill self-belief in a student?"

Answer: Provide courses that will provide the following:
1) the **EXPERIENCE of acceptance and validation from peers** whether it be from their friends or totally different groups of kids,
2) that will enable each student to learn the basics of communication skills—verbal and non-verbal, listening skills, attitude training, and people skills, and
3) the opportunity to **learn their own "specialness"** through discovering their passion.

Everyone lives their lives from their own individual framework, a set of guiding principles they may not even be consciously aware of. These principles are formed from childhood experiences, family interactions, schooling, friendships, religious and ethnic training.

Having our actions come from a framework consisting of honesty, integrity, and morality may explain why we react in a negative way to actions not consistent with those three principles, and there is a lot more to consider.

We have to ask ourselves: What is my personal role in the world? How great is my human compassion? Is the phrase "Peace on earth; good will to all" merely a saying or is there meaning within those words? Catherine of Siena said, "Proclaim the truth and do not be silent through fear."

Belief in justice, equality, peace, and community is a strong, solid common ground on which to start. The students make the choices; the students decide on their own value systems.

In today's world what numbs the mind are irresponsible affluence, unfair judgments of people, and malicious untruths. "Lying is done with words and also with silence." - Adrienne Rich.

In many of today's classrooms and playgrounds, too many kids are following what they see people they admire do on TV and on their own streets. Too many kids are being bullied. Too many bullied kids end up thinking they are worthless, their self-esteem destroyed. **To be made invisible is to be made impotent. Marginalization can be worse than death.**

These reasons are why every educator should read this book. Through actual classroom experiences, students experience acceptance by their peers in situations where they never would have been able to get to know one another. The nerds, the brainiacs, the sport heroes, the tough guys, the potential drop-outs, rich and poor get to experience first-hand, from their peers, their own specialness. That's why you should read this book.

Table of Contents

CHAPTER ONE: BACKGROUND
WHAT'S THE PROBLEM?

After many years of teaching, Abby Foster finally retired. She had worked hard and spent almost every night of the school year, even school vacations, either correcting papers or creating what she felt were exciting lesson plans for her students.

She wanted her students to succeed and many did, but not everyone. It was the "not everyone" kids that preyed on her mind. Too many kids seemed unmotivated; some developed an "entitled" attitude; some dropped out of school before graduation.

She wanted to know why. What is the common denominator(s) that determines success or lack of success for students?

Shortly after her retirement, an ad appeared in the paper for a part-time adult school English teacher for high school dropouts, ages 18 to 25. She applied and was immediately hired. She believed that this was the perfect laboratory to study kids who had chosen to drop out of high school. What are the commonalities that caused students to drop out? Are there solutions? Could there be solutions?

If there was anyone at VoTech Adult High School who genuinely cared for her students, it was Abby Foster. She was a dedicated teacher, had gotten great evaluations by her department chairman every year when she taught high school English, and she had great relationships with her peers as well as with the kids in her classes. She loved her job!

Nevertheless, she hurt whenever she lost a student to the streets, to a gang or to a life of poverty, because she knows that a child's chances of success in life are slim once they choose to drop out of school. Many end up in jail; many join gangs.

She saw this job as an opportunity to work at this special adult school for high school dropouts. Maybe she could find a solution - a way to help prevent future dropouts. She truly wanted to make a difference; but, as the semester progressed, she was beginning to doubt herself and her value to the school.

Again, her students were already dropouts. This was their second chance. From her reading of *Winning the Brain Race* by Kearns and Doyle, Abby was particularly aware that in high schools around the country today, there are underachieving, unmotivated students who graduate each year with minimal reading and writing skills. She didn't want her students to have minimal skills.

The fact that America's public schools graduate 700,000 functionally illiterate students every year, and 700,000 more drop out is upsetting to any teacher who cares about her students. Four out of five young adults in a recent survey couldn't summarize the main point of a newspaper article, or read a bus schedule, or figure their change from a restaurant bill, according to the authors.

This year, a number of Abby's students were already failing in spite of the time she devoted to her preparation for class and her individualized work with the students. For such a dedicated teacher, she felt she was not making a difference. Unless something changed dramatically, almost a dozen of her students were not going to graduate with their class.

In her melancholy state of mind, Abby thought to herself, "Maybe it's time for me to move on." "Maybe a solution doesn't exist; maybe I should mind my own business!"

She reminisced about her first year of teaching many decades ago and how she became interested in "disaffected" kids, kids who were bright but just didn't care. As the "newbie" on the staff, she was given what was considered the worst kids, the kids no one wanted to teach, the kids who already had police records, the kids who didn't do homework, pay attention, or even care about school. Her first class was a group of sophomores, average age, 17 instead of the usual sophomore age of 15, and consisted of 28 boys, 2 girls; and they were tough kids!

She recalled how, as the year progressed, she grew to love this roguish group of kids. If they were interested in the topic being taught, she found them to be bright, mischievous, independent, and hard working.

Getting them excited about reading *Silas Marner* and *Julius Caesar* and learning infinitives, gerunds, participles, etc. was easy as long as the material was relevant to them, was fun, and involved no put-downs. Having them help one another was even more rewarding. They learned the material more solidly by helping each another, and they enjoyed the satisfaction of having made a difference in their fellow peers' successes.

Abby's second major encounter with "disaffected" kids came when she was contracted to teach the teachers at a county juvenile detention center. She recalls her shock the day she arrived at the center and discovered the teachers had quit—all of them!

Her revised contract called for her to teach a four-day course, *Success Strategies*, to the teenagers incarcerated at the detention center. "How hard could that be?" she wondered to herself.

The purpose of the course is to teach the teens the importance of choices, attitude, nonverbal communication, and interviewing skills - all done in a fun, fast-paced way.

When Abby was asked if the program was a success, she responded with a resounding NO! And she explained why.

The procedures she had to perform before she even met with the teens should have forewarned her about her upcoming adventure.

After signing in, Abby was directed to the visitor's room with her piles of booklets straining her arms and was asked to remove all of the staples from the two sets of booklets and the plastic spiral binding from another. She was told that the inmates could use these sharp implements for self mutilation or as weapons. She understood.

With the books readied for the kids, Abby then had to return to her car and stow her purse in the trunk, bringing only a form of ID with her into the building which was then exchanged for a badge. No pencils or pens allowed. Abby's keys were hung at the receptionist's desk.

She was escorted through the metal detector and heavy metal doors, all controlled by the guards in the enclosed glass booth filled with monitors.

The classroom was like any other—desks, blackboard, chairs—nothing unusual, except it was devoid of any decorations, not even chalk. It was stark.

Shortly after they arrived, in marched the first class of boys in line from the shortest to the tallest. Seven young men walked into the room preceded by a large burly guard and followed by two more large men. Seven kids, three guards, two Center employees, my partner and me. Seven adults/seven kids! Abby had worked with "at risk" kids before, but this experience was different. *Surly, angry, defiant, unresponsive* are the best descriptors that immediately came to mind when she saw the teens. They totally avoided eye contact.

"Please open your books to page 10" evoked looks of disgust, looks that silently screamed, "Don't bother me, Lady?" Abby continued undeterred.

The lightness of the material slowly seeped into the melancholy of a few who actually began to pay attention and almost looked as if they were enjoying the material.

During the discussion of nonverbal communications, Abby asked the class if they were aware that if they see a friend in the hall, their eyebrows briefly flicker upward, then return to their normal position - an involuntary sign of recognition; however, if they see a cute gal they have a crush on, their eyebrows may stay elevated - a sign of interest.

Most seemed to enjoy this information. Abby believes that information was the cause of the most unusual question that took her by surprise. After almost zero response, suddenly a young man thrusts his hand in the air and yells,

"Miss, When you were young, were you a hooker?" She detected no disrespect, only curiosity. His classmates did look up to hear her response.

Abby replied, "No, just a teacher." And he seemed fine with that. No one chortled or reacted in a surprised manner at the question.

Abby then showed them how powerful their minds are by holding a ball dangling from a string. She told them that she could "think" it to move. She asked them to tell her the direction they would like the object to move.

She explained that by thinking about the direction of the ball in her mind and moving her eyes in an up-and-down, back-and-forth, or circular position, the tiny muscles in her fingers would unconsciously move the ball. Most people can replicate the experiment. It was merely a demonstration to make the point about the power of their minds.

The downside to this display was the reaction of one of the most vocal boys in the class. Every time Abby called on someone, he would yell, "Don't look in her eyes. She'll control your mind." Initially, she thought he was kidding. He wasn't.

The next day when Abby returned, the same boy demanded, "Why are you back?" She was surprised by his harsh tone.

She said, "I like you guys." Another mistake. He spent the entire period proving how unlikable he is. Finally, Abby gave in and said, "Okay, I don't like you." And he was fine.

He wanted to know where her partner was. Abby explained that she was taking care of her grandchild and would be back on Tuesday. He didn't believe her. He said, "She's never coming back. Teachers don't come back here!"

Now Abby was getting a bit of insight into what was happening. He expected to be let down. He expected people not to like him, and to make sure he was right, he made himself a royal pain in the tush.

And this is why Abby feels the program was not a success. She believes that these kids need someone trained in this material who can work with them one-on-one every day, not an outsider who first has to gain their trust, and then try to impact this fluid population. They need some stability. They need someone who cares about them.

Abby also slowly learned that in some of her classes, a leader in the class controlled the kids - by a glance, a look, an action that the others immediately understood.

In one class, a very handsome, charismatic young man was an absolute sweet-heart. He loved everything Abby presented, was totally cooperative, and sweet-talked the daylights out of her, and she bought in – hook, line, and sinker – until she finally saw the surreptitious "look." The "look" he furtively shot at his classmates if they were doing something – like participating – that he didn't want them to be doing, and the look was responded to immediately. For example, if Abby said"turn to page 45," she finally realized that no one touched his book until Mr. Sweet-talk touched his.

One day Abby asked one of the guards if he ever became attached to any the kids. He responded very strongly, "Not anymore!" He explained that early on he had become attached to some of the kids and gotten "burned." He wouldn't explain further.

Some of the kids did touch Abby's heart; some were scary; some so defiant that they made teaching very difficult.

The guard explained that these kids are "players," street-smart kids who have mastered the art of manipulation. He added that those who aren't players are either brain-fried or illiterate. "That's why they don't open the book when you tell them to. They can't read." Abby hadn't thought about that.

She also asked the guard why the kids were here. He replied, "Murder, rape, drugs, armed robbery." Wow!

Does Abby believe these kids are throwaways, impossible to save? She does believe that those who have permanent brain damage will probably spend the rest of their lives in a protected area, or perhaps it should be said, "hopefully spend their lives confined in some way," because they can kill and maim and not really be responsible because of their diminished capacity.

The extremes are the brain-fried and the manipulators. If Abby compares them to a barrel of fruit, she would say there are some rotten apples, i.e., throwaways; and there are ones on the verge of turning sour, that, if taken under a strong caring person's wing, could turn out to be effective members of society.

Abby is very aware of the numbers. According to some experts, we are failing almost half of the teenage population who either drop out, graduate as illiterates, or develop an attitude of "entitlement." To prevent too many apples from rotting, she believes teachers have to help out in the field—they have to nurture the crop.

Hearing her kids about to enter her classroom, Abby snaps out of her reverie as she watches the students take their seats.

With a start, she thinks, "I wonder if what I learned from my first class decades ago and from my Juvenile Detention kids would apply to today's kids?"

"The world is different today," she knows. "Technology, transportation, entertainment, even foods have changed," she realizes as she sees her class settle in, take their books out, and stow their phones where they cannot be seen.

Then it struck her: "**What has not changed over the years is human nature.** A Theory of Human Motivation by American psychologist Abraham Maslow is still a highly regarded source of information for determining human needs. His Hierarchy of Needs is still in effect: **1) Survival Needs** (food, water, clean air, and shelter), **2) Safety Needs** (mental and physical), **3) Social Needs** (people: friends, and family), **4) Esteem Needs** (acceptance, validation, self-belief), all leading to **5) Self-Actualization** (making a difference in the world).

All five areas are as relevant today as they were when Maslow wrote about them in 1943.

With a tingle of giddiness and a feeling of hope, Abby begins her class and enjoys the feelings of excitement and promise build as she interacts with her students.

She knows what she has to do!

With only a few months left before graduation, Abby decides to confront the problem head on. She will personally study, interview, and write a case study for each "at risk" student in order to determine what their mindset is and what their intentions are insofar as graduating with their class. She hopes she will learn something that she could use in the future. Even more, she hopes she can keep these kids in school so they can graduate.

But first, she has something she intends to do in order to make the interview meaningful and not rote. She wants to make sure that each student is aware of her recognition of what is special about them, that this is not a meaningless prying into their psyches.

She challenges herself to write a brief case study about each student that concerns her. The format is always the same: what she sees as positives about their personality or abilities or attitude or interaction with classmates - anything that she regards as a plus.

At the end of the case study, she decides to include an area of recommendation, something that would benefit the student in the long-run.

Because of time constraints, Abby limits her case studies to those kids she feels are at risk of dropping out or failing out of school. Not being a neighborhood school, most of the students don't hang out or even live near one another. If, perchance, a student feels "left out" because they didn't get a case study written about them, she will make the time to include them.
All interviews are done outside the classroom and are not shared with their classmates.

Before the interviews with the students begin, Abby studies the personalities in her class and writes "general impressions" case studies on those students who are the most challenging.

Her intent is to find commonalities, positive traits and conditions to build on. She keeps in mind questions such as

1. Is there anything, words and/or deeds, that all people respond to?
2. What, if any, commonalities are there regarding interacting with students?
3. What actions can students (or anyone) adopt to feel better about themselves and/or others?
4. What human relation skills should everyone adopt?
5. What's the importance of non-verbal communication?
6. How important is listening?
7. Which ethics are most important to adopt?
8. Does everyone have to adopt the same ethic?
9. What part does belief play in a person's behavior, actions and reactions?
10. Besides Shelter and Safety, what's the most important thing(s) a person needs to succeed in life?

As a result of her interviews and case studies, Abby has come up with a list of what she referred to as The Laws of Human Nature. She developed a Baker's Dozen list that she feels is applicable to everyone.

Her first subject is Miguel.

CHAPTER TWO: BASIC HUMAN LAWS

Human Nature Law #1:
SHOW RESPECT TO GET RESPECT

At the beginning of the semester Abby heard from her fellow teachers about a young man who has been labeled a "real trouble maker" in other classes. Abby's experience with Miguel was totally different.

On the first day of class, Abby walked into the room and immediately saw a tall, lanky young man holding a very short girl's sneaker in his hand, her foot attached. She was hobbling to maintain her upright position. Abby ran behind her to keep her from falling and realized, "This must be Miguel." It was.

The look in his eyes and the mischievousness of his expression told Abby that he was not a threat—maybe a pest but not a threat.

After weeks of observing the young man, Abby wrote her impressions of Miguel:

> He has Michael Jordon's low key, teasing manner and warm, laughing eyes. I envy his laid-back personality. He could care less about making an impression. He's just Miguel, and he takes life and himself lightly--unless he is shown disrespect. Overall, he has a wonderful attitude.

> He loves to tease, especially the tiny little gal in his class who is one-half his size. He threatens to send the smurfs to beat her up. She gets mad, and he keeps needling her—and she enjoys his attention.

> One day in the middle of class, Miguel got up from his desk, walked to the front of the room and patted me on my head. Startled, I looked at him, and he whispered, "Miss, your hair was sticking up."

> With hesitation, I stammered, "Thank you, Miguel."

Another time while everyone was quietly working in class, he yelled out with excited exuberance, "Miss, I know who you look like!"

"Who, Miguel? I asked."

"Santa's mom!"

"Thank you, Miguel," to which he sweetly uttered under his breath, "She's a cute little old lady."

This 6-foot 6 gentle giant is a delightful, spirited, handsome young man. He has a wonderful sense of humor. He's kind. He is a tease. He is a talker. He has personality galore. What he does not have is tolerance for anyone, including his teachers, who do not show him respect. When shown respect, he becomes a devotee.

Many of these high school dropouts have done things they should not have done; some have paid their dues through the penal system; some are awaiting their trials, and some still may not be clear between the boundaries of right and wrong, acceptable and unacceptable; appropriate and inappropriate.

Miguel is an example of an exuberant young man who at times is inappropriate, but he has good intentions. Abby believes that what made the difference in his behavior in her class was showing him respect as she expected respect from him--in spite of his sometimes- unusual behavior.

LESSON LEARNED: SHOW RESPECT TO GET RESPECT! People mirror other people. If they see hatred, they show hate. If they see respect, they show respect. "The Children's Creed" contains perfect examples.

CHILD'S CREED
CHILDREN LEARN WHAT THEY LIVE

If a child lives with criticism, he learns to condemn.
If a child lives with acceptance, he learns to love.
If a child lives with hostility, he learns to fight.
If a child lives with approval, he learns to like himself.
If a child lives with fear, he learns to be apprehensive.
If a child lives with recognition, he learns to have a goal.
If a child lives with pity, he learns to be sorry for himself.
If a child lives with fairness, he learns what justice is.
If a child lives with jealously, he learns to feel guilty.
If a child lives with honesty, he learns what truth is.
If a child lives with encouragement, he learns to be confident.
If a child lives with tolerance, he learns to be patient.
If a child lives with praise, he learns to be appreciative.
If a child lives with security, he learns to have faith in himself.
If a child lives with friendliness, he learns that a world is a nice place to live.
- Author Unknown

Human Nature Law #2:
BE NONJUDGMENTAL

On Abby's first cold January evening at the adult school for dropouts, she watched the young adults file into her classroom. The males were dressed in what looked like expensive jackets and either knitted caps pulled down over their ears or doo-rags or baseball caps on sideways. Although the room was toasty warm, they never took off their jackets for the entire class period. She later learned they feared their jackets would be stolen.

The females dressed provocatively--tight jeans, low-cut tops or tight sweaters, and, for the most part, they did not smile, at least not at her.

Abby's first impression was: *Here are some really rough, tough kids.* What she did not know were the stories each "at risk" student had. She had to be careful not to equate what she saw and/or heard with any impression of "bad." Here are a few other "first impressions."

• One of the first topics raised in class that evening was how fast they could get Abby's car to a "chop shop," a term Abby was unfamiliar with but quickly understood in context.

• As Abby was leaving the building her first night, in the parking lot all she could hear was the "f" word, "f------ this" and "f------ that," over and over. Finally, one of the students saw her and screamed at his friends, "Hey guys, watch your "f------ language;" my "f------English teacher is here." He meant well, and it did strike her funny, though she did not show her reaction.

• One of the first essays Abby read after the first night ended concluded with the following sentence: *"I shot him three times and got four years."* EEK!

• In one of Abby's classes was an 18-year-old girl, who has a five year old and a two year old--two different fathers, and she lives with her mom--and she is a real sweetheart!!

What Abby saw, read, and heard that first night made "being nonjudgmental" a very difficult concept to practice. As the semester progressed, however, she found all of the above words and behaviors to have no bearing at all on who they are or the probability of their potential success.

How they were treated or their perception of how they were treated, and how well they were doing had a far greater bearing on their success or lack thereof.

One young man did jail time for selling drugs. Was he a bad kid? Abby didn't think so after she heard his story

He "tawks" tough - a "project" accent. He's a white kid with dreadlocks and baggy pants, and he has survived.

When he was 12 years old, his single mother had a breakdown, and Omar became the breadwinner for the family. How could he best feed them all? --$5 an hour at McDonalds (a job he was too young to get) or $500 a night on the corner selling drugs? He did what worked for him at the time, and he landed in jail. Poor choice, but how was he to know?

What's special about Omar? He's kind, gentle, caring, sweet - a truly good, loyal, nice person unwittingly put into a bad situation for which he has paid the piper.

One day Abby was admonishing the class about keeping the room neat because the day teacher had complained again. In response to her exasperation, she heard a soft voice from the side of the room whisper, "Miss, ya wanus to take care of her?" asked Omar. Oh my!

He plays by the rules he learned as a child and as a child in jail.

What does Omar want to do with his life? He wants to counsel kids. Would he be good at it? You bet he would! He has sensitivity, sincerity, kindness, and meaningful experiences on which to draw. With the help of someone who believes in him, he may make it.

I hope he has an opportunity to travel that path. He deserves it, and he could really make a difference in the lives of potential lawbreaking teens. What a difference a a caring adult could make in Omar's life!

Some stories these young adults have experienced are almost unbelievable. Read about what Danny had to say about a can of soda.

The class was doing extemporaneous talks, which means Abby says a word, and they have to tell her a story about the word. She pointed to Danny and said, "soda." The soft spoken, reticent, introspective young man abruptly stood up and said vigorously, "I have a story" and proceeded with a tale that tore at everyone's heart.

"I went to the refrigerator to get a soda. My Dad came in and said, 'You better replace that. It's your mom's last soda.'

'I will,' I said, knowing she wasn't expected home for a couple of hours.

Before I even finished my soda, my mother came in, went to the refrigerator and yelled, 'Who took my soda?' "

Danny immediately assured her he would replace it right away.

"Now," he paused and said softly, "My dad loves to buy my mom rings with pretty stones. She wears rings on all of her fingers."

As Danny continued, he described how his mother with fingers on both hands bedecked with jeweled rings, pulled back her right fist and smashed him in the face, the rings tearing into his cheeks. His head snapped to the right, and her left fist tore into the right side of his face with ferocity. He slid down the wall to avoid further strikes, and she immediately started kicking him in the head with her spike-heeled shoes. His father ran in and pulled her off of him.

Danny ran, which angered his father who ran after him and attempted to punch him. Danny jumped out of the way, and his father smashed his fist into the wall, jamming his wrist. He was ten times angrier now because he had bowling that night.

Danny quietly stated, "He still rolled 200."

The class questioned the veracity of his story, "Your mom wouldn't do that! Oh, come on!"

With eyes wide open and emotion still clutching his mind, Danny assured the class, "Oh yes she did! This happened!" and everyone believed him.

All for a can of soda! Danny related the story with emotion yet acceptance, as if "wow!" but "no big deal."

An aside: Danny had missed a few classes earlier in the semester. Why? Abby learned that he had been treated in the hospital for attempted suicide. Would anyone wonder why? Again, what you see and hear may not be "what is."

LESSON LEARNED: BE NONJUDGMENTAL. Accept your students as they are, and then provide the atmosphere for them to grow in a positive manner. Everybody has a story, and most will remain unknown to a teacher.

What you see and hear may not be what is. Clothes and words make an initial impression, but, having an impression and making a judgment are two different things. Judgment can cloud one's vision and frequently close doors.

"Accepting" a student or friend is a higher form of "being nonjudgmental." Making a judgment is responding to a stereotype in our own minds--doo-rags means "bad." Non-acceptance--being offended--is a personal response to a behavior or to words we believe to be offensive or wrong

Unfortunately, it is usually easier and perhaps safer to see faults in others rather than strengths. That is human nature. Finding a fault in someone else makes us feel better, for example, "He's fatter, louder, messier, etc.," if we can consider ourselves a wee bit superior by comparison.

Human Nature Law #3:
SEEK THE STRENGTHS IN EVERY STUDENT

- Help every student recognize his or her specialness.
- Remember that everyone desperately wants to feel special.
- See the invisible tattoo on every student's forehead that reads: **"PLEASE MAKE ME FEEL IMPORTANT!"**

Show Abby a difficult teenager or young adult, and she will show you someone who doesn't feel appreciated and/or special. Get to know the person and you cannot help but see something that is distinctive about that person. It could be a sense of humor or warmth when dealing with a peer or sincerity or just a sparkle in their eyes.

Not everyone will fit the image of the perfect student, yet each possesses strengths, although he or she may not be aware of such distinctions.

Tall, angular, lithe, George commands a room when he enters. He non-verbally demands the attention of the group. He dresses impeccably. Abby tells him he should put together a portfolio and go to a modeling agency. She can definitely picture him on the pages of a Lord & Taylor circular.

George is not unaware of his attractiveness. He hits on girls like Babe Ruth hit home runs.

Underneath the good looks and confident attitude runs a river of anger, deep and well hidden. In response to a question in class, "What don't you like about your life right now?" Abby heard a barely audible but clearly angry response, "white people," which she didn't take personally, because she believes he doesn't put her in that large pool. She thinks she slides by in the category of teacher without color, and he knows she really cares for him.

Another invisible aspect of George is his talent. He writes metaphorically. His words elicit pictures from the reader's mind. And he has the ability to tie them together without overkill. He is a naturally talented writer.

George is tough but vulnerable. He eyes, laughing one minute, unsure the next, give him away. He can be arrogant and act as if rules do not apply to him, yet Abby sees a caring, kind, young man under the facade of glamour and power he surrounds himself with. She sees a young man who, like most of us, needs respect and attention and needs to be a success in life. Beyond the bravado lies a sweetheart of a young man.

With George's ambition and natural abilities, his people skills, attitude, and confidence, Abby believes he will succeed in whatever field he chooses.

LESSONS LEARNED: SEEK THE STRENGTHS IN EVERY STU-DENT. When Abby pointed out his strengths via a character sketch she had written about him, George was so surprised and delighted, he brought in his parents and aunts so they could meet her and see what she had written about him. (Three years after Abby had met his family at graduation, she read in the local paper the story of his stepmother's brutal slaying by his father.) A caring teacher, counselor, or mentor would be invaluable for George!

One student who was encouraged only to look for the positives in others wrote: "The final and probably most important skill that I learned in this class was to only look for the positive in people. Because we were instructed to write down only positive things on our evaluation cards, picking out the good in people instead of bad has become second nature to me. This skill not only makes other people feel better, but it also reflects itself on my own disposition. When a person learns to see the positive in other people it brings a much more peaceful, optimistic outlook to the rest of the world around them." - Alessandra M.

Part of the problem in evaluating ourselves is we frequently do not see our own strengths; seeing strengths in others is easier than seeing them in ourselves. While a teacher may be aware of her student's needed areas of improvement, she may find that it is actually fun to seek the positives in them and in others she meets and let them know what she sees and why. The "why" validates the compliment.

Human Nature Law #4:
PROVIDE A SAFE ATMOSPHERE

Stephen Covey, in his book, *The Seven Habits of Highly Effective People*, talks about an eye doctor who was examining a patient who had complained that he couldn't see clearly. The eye doctor gave him his own glasses and said, "Try mine. They have worked for me for the last 25 years." The patient still could not see.

Abby encourages teachers to remember that each student brings with them his or her own prescriptive lenses through which they view the world. Everyone has different levels of vision--different prescriptions--according to their backgrounds and experiences in life. No one prescription fits all.

In order to provide a safe atmosphere for students, Abby believes a person must keep in mind that what they see and how they see may be different from what we may see and how we may see it.

Out of Abby's three classes one semester, one young man stands out--or rather *leaps* out in her mind. Timaro is that person--a real sweetheart! He is a delightful 24-year-old bundle of explosive energy that ignites at the slightest provocation--noise in the classroom, an "A" on a paper, an idea. He's like a "thought" jack-in-the-box or a drunken kangaroo--Abby never knew what was going to pop up next.

When he receives an "A" on a paper--and he receives many of them--he jumps up, goes to the other teachers in the room and enthusiastically demands, "See that! What does that say?" He is so proud, as well he should be.

He receives the "A's" because he has the ability to write from his heart. He also receives a second, usually lower grade for spelling and grammar, but that grade does not dampen his enthusiasm. He is conscientious and does all of his work. His enthusiasm is so refreshing and fun to watch!

The aspect of Timaro that Abby most admires is his sincerity. As he writes, so does he speak--from his heart, and he is easily wounded.

One day Abby was announcing her "perfect students" which merely means those who had all of their work in. Even though she had read Timaro's latest essay, he hadn't turned in the final copy; therefore, his name was not included in her announcement. She knew immediately that her omission had hurt him. "But, Miss, you saw my paper!" Abby wished she could take back her words.

That incident revealed to her how hard Timaro works to be his best so he can get recognition for his efforts.

He confided in her that his father had always told him he wouldn't amount to anything--in variations that Timaro interpreted in the same way--he was a nothing and would always be a nothing.

Perhaps his father had been practicing tough love, hoping to motivate Timaro; but his method and assessment had an adverse effect on his son.

Timaro is unique. He is a tall, thin, handsome young man who wears his hair in dreadlocks adorned with five small white puca shells tied into his hair. Each shell represents a special person in his life--one being his child, another his "Boo"--his special young lady, and another his mother.

Timaro is loud, outgoing, funny, and kind. He can be sitting quietly working and suddenly Abby will hear a startling loud "Miss!" even if she's standing right next to him. He has a question or impulse and acts on it immediately. This could be related to his energy level. He cannot be still for long. He could possibly be hyperactive. He apologizes if he feels he has been out of line-- talking too much. He'll hush up others if he feels they have been out of line.

The class loves him. He can be outrageous, yet he is always kind. He'll tease Kareema and those around him, and they always respond with a laugh or a smile. He has his own seat but frequently changes in order to make another classmate feel special.

Timaro has definite leadership qualities, which just have to be pointed in the right direction. From what Abby hears him say, at least two major factors have molded him: his father's constant invalidation/criticism and the streets, which have taught him some harsh lessons. He has been, and is, in trouble with the law. Is locking him up the correct way to go for what he has done? The easy-going, outgoing exterior covers a deeply sensitive, genuinely nice person. Prison could drown that kind, inner person. Constructive direction would free the potential this young man possesses.

Timaro has the enthusiasm, the brains, and the sensitivity to be an outstanding teacher. Abby would love to see that happen. His creativity, his energy level, his leadership qualities, his sensitivity to others, his kindness, and his experiences in life all combine to potentially make him a positive influence on others.

Timaro will always have a special place in Abby's heart, and she hopes that all of his positive qualities will be given an opportunity to shine. He is one who could help make the world a better place in which to live.

There are two kinds of scars: external, which will heal; and internal, which leaves a scar. Ridicule from peers or teachers can leave scars. A safe atmosphere means a place where one can be himself without fear of ridicule.

A "safe atmosphere" does not preclude "boundaries." What a safe atmosphere does is allow a student to be himself. Providing this safety infers respect, non-judgment, boundaries, and acceptance.

LESSON LEARNED: PROVIDE A SAFE ATMOSPHERE. By providing a safe place for students, they are unafraid to show their strengths and build upon them, especially with the guidance of a caring teacher.

A safe atmosphere can be set up by someone who truly believes in the concept of making everyone feel important, no matter what generation they represent. Because this concept of feeling important and accepted is the unconscious wish of everybody, it is difficult and uncomfortable to operate under any other canopy.

Human Nature Law #5:
KNOW THAT YOU CANNOT NOT COMMUNICATE, but what you think you see or hear may not be what is.

One young man in the back of Abby's class would never look at her or respond when she asked him a question. She believed he totally disliked her, but he never caused any trouble. He spoke to no one.

One day Abby was handing out papers and was near his desk when she heard "Psst! Miss! Look at this, but don't say nothing." He handed her a paper, which she put into her briefcase and took home with her.

His paper contained a poem about a girl he was deeply in love with. The poem was moving, tender, and beautifully written. Abby used post-it notes to point out what was particularly and specifically good about the poem and handed it back the next day. She was certain she had won him over.

Wrong! Again, he avoided looking at her and never responded when she spoke to him.

Weeks later, near the end of the semester, Abby heard another, "Psst! Miss! Look at this, but don't say nothing." He handed her a paper, which she read while standing next to his desk. This poem brought tears to her eyes, which he witnessed. The poem was about his attempt to end his life because his girl had left him.

When Abby went home, she again used post-it notes to comment on the excellence of his writing. She went on-line and found poetry writing contests, all of which she printed and gave him the next day.

When she returned his paper with the numerous post-it notes and the packet of contest forms, he took it, looked away, and never spoke to her again—ever.

This young man has the ability to express himself beautifully through poetry. The problem is Abby will never know if he uses his gift. Had he had the opportunity to work with someone who believed in him and encouraged him, he may have opened up. He may have been persuaded to utilize his writing ability.

Misinterpreting nonverbal communication is easy to do.

One young, vastly pregnant gal looked at Abby each day with disdain. She rolled her tee shirt up exposing her huge swollen belly and looked at Abby with the "Okay Miss, what are you going to do about it?" look on her face.

Abby never reacted.

After class one night she came to Abby's podium to ask a question about the final exam, when suddenly she bent over as she experienced a sharp contraction. Abby put her arm around her (forbidden action), and the gal instantly relaxed. Her baby was due in three weeks, and she wanted to know about the final exam, also scheduled in three weeks.

After that event, she came up every class period, and finally told Abby how scared she was because in three weeks, when the baby was born, she was going to be kicked out of the shelter.

Abby asked about her parents. She responded, "They won't take me in because I'm too black."

Her comment shocked Abby. Who knew the mental anguish this young gal was going through every single day! Some adult - a caring adult, a preacher, a guidance counselor, someone, could have provided this young lady with guidance and validation.

LESSON LEARNED: YOU CANNOT <u>NOT</u> COMMUNICATE. The poet's body language told Abby he did not want her to pay attention to him. His actions told her an entirely different story.

The pregnant young lady also nonverbally told Abby to "stay away," and in reality, she responded to being comforted, a response she probably didn't expect to experience.

Abby learned to go with her instincts. She learned that a non-response is also a response. She learned that what she viewed as a look of disdain was probably a fear of rejection posture.

As Stephen Covey says, "Try to understand before you are understood." Misunderstanding someone else's demeanor, tone of voice, or words is so easy to do.

Human Nature Law #6:
SET HIGH EXPECTATIONS

Another young man in the class was not only unaware of his gifts, but also he was convinced he was incompetent:

The first impression Abby had of Jack was that of a quiet, pensive young man. He is one who stays removed from the group until he analyzes the situation and feels secure enough to participate. He looks before he leaps.

What he doesn't know is that he is one of the most special students in the group. He is sincere. He is fun. He is personable. And he is bright, a lot brighter than he gives himself credit for.

Jack regularly pulls the Marc Anthony at Caesar's funeral act. "I have come not to praise Caesar but to bury him," and then very cleverly lets the crowd understand Caesar's greatness. With Jack, it's "Miss, I can't do this. I can't write. I can't. I just can't do it!" He'll repeat this mantra numerous times, and then hands in a paper that is written quite nicely.

For the next assignment, he starts all over again. "I can't do this, Miss. You have to understand; I just can't do it."

Jack is a genuinely nice person. He picks and chooses his friends carefully and, Abby would imagine, is loyal to a fault.

He also has a wonderful sense of humor. One day Abby stepped into the hall for a few minutes, returned, and there was Jack standing there with a devilish grin on his face. "Missing anything, Miss?" he asked. Abby looked at him blankly as he began to unload his pockets--her stopwatch, bell, clicker, pencil, pen, marker--and she hadn't even noticed. He chuckled as he left the room.

Jack is good with people. He's kind, gentle, sensitive, easy-going. He's good looking. He's fun and funny. Abby could easily see him owning his own deli or someplace where he'd deal with people on a regular basis. That's his strength--his understanding of people and his ability to relate to them and make them feel good. Whatever he chooses, Abby hopes he remembers that he is one very special young man, and he can do whatever he wants to do.

LESSON LEARNED: SET HIGH EXPECTATIONS. The story is true about the new teacher who thought the locker list from 140-160 was the list of IQs in her class and she treated them accordingly, and they performed accordingly. What she didn't know was that she had the lowest performing group at that grade level. Because she treated them as if they were bright, set high expectations, they acted as if they were bright.

Human Nature Law #7:
MAKE SINCERITY YOUR #1 PRIORITY

An essential component of every relationship is sincerity. The sincerity of the teacher is paramount. Students can pick out a phony in very short order, especially street-smart kids who have "been around." Trying to be "one of the guys" does not work, and it affects the students' perception of the teacher's sincerity.

Abby had a very handsome young man in her class who happened to be a delightful con man. A few weeks passed before she realized how frequently she had been duped. For example, one speaking assignment required him to sell a product. He chose cologne. On his evaluation card, Abby wrote, "I don't have a clue what he's saying." I knew it wasn't cologne he was selling. I could tell by the response of the class that it had to be something illegal. When Abby challenged him, he smiled broadly and said, "Okay, I'll sell ice cream."

Same scenario--couldn't understand a thing he said. He was pitching drugs and having a ball doing it, especially when he knew that I didn't know the terminology.

What's so special about this?

This young man's mental adroitness is incredible. He relishes the spotlight, doesn't allow criticism (Abby's) to dampen his spirits and generally maintains a positive attitude. His stature and extraordinary good looks facilitate his success at the con game, a phrase Abby uses with affection.

Those are the positives. While Abby doesn't want to encourage him to be a "flim flam" man, she does want to encourage him to use his talents in a positive way. But how? His ability to speak "around her" would be useful in negotiating or selling.

Success will probably elude this young man as long as he lacks sincerity. He is bright. He does have charm. He does have warmth. He doesn't have sincerity; therefore, he cannot be trusted and won't be trusted once people get past the facade one time.

Abby learned that a teacher can quickly learn the lingo used for drugs and lifestyle, but she believes that "Playing dumb" can work to a teacher's advantage. Anyone can learn a lot by being "out of it" or "not cool." Anyone can play dumb and still be sincere.

Trying to sound and talk like the students does not work to a teacher's advantage. It is okay to be "older" and "not cool." Attempts to be one of them is each teacher's own desire to be accepted. They just have to get over that!

LESSON LEARNED: MAKE SINCERITY YOUR #1 PRIORITY.
As important as it is to encourage a student to be him- or herself, it is equally important for the teacher to be himself or herself. Someone in their 20's working with teens is a decade older and already has some "dated" singing idols and music favorites. Whether a teacher is in their 30's, 40's, 50's or higher, it's okay to be who they are regardless of the generation to which they belong.

Each generation is unique, and those from other age groups who try to "fit in" by using "hip" jargon may sound foolish. Be sincere to your students as well as to yourself.

Sincerity with others and sincerity to oneself is even more effective when cushioned with warmth. In her book, *Your Child's Self-Esteem*, Dorothy Corkhill Briggs says that the most important factor for a person's self-esteem is the degree of warmth experienced by the child, rather than any particular techniques of child training. Warmth is an integral part of making a person feel important; it is an integral part of feeling accepted.

Anyone can master human relation skills, but they are merely tools of manipulation if lacking sincerity.

Human Nature Law #8:
BE SENSITIVE

Sensitivity is one characteristic of the students that Abby had noticed numerous times when dealing with the "at risk" population. She realized that once they trust you, they become very sensitive to how you act and react, especially when they feel your "sensitivity" toward them.

As part of a *Discover Your Passion* assignment, Abby had the students list words that they believed described themselves. Almost everyone wrote the word "nice." Some chose words such as "loyal," "shy," "outgoing," "talented," plus many more.

Primarily, they wanted Abby to know they were nice people in spite of what has happened to them, what they had done, and where they are currently.

Abby then asked them to write three words they would like to have describe them. For example, she said, "I would like to have people describe me as "skinny." She had said that same line for 16 years teaching her *Discover Your Passion* course to adults, and people always chuckled and went on with their assignment.

This time the class stopped and looked at her. One boy said, "Why you wanna be skinny, Miss? You got a husband."

Another boy said, "You look fine, Miss."

Now Abby was embarrassed. She was only trying to be funny.

Then the last young man said, "Miss, ain't you heard that thick chicks is better than skinny ones?"

Abby loved it. It's all perspective! She realized she doesn't have a weight problem; she's just a thick chick. Because they had accepted her, they were sensitive to her being hurt in any way.

Abby believes that showing the same sensitivity about their challenges in life will do more for their self-esteem than anything anyone could do.

One invaluable lesson Abby learned about the importance of being sensitive came as a result of her less-than-neutral response to a student from Columbia who said it was most important that he have a hot meal on the table when he gets home from work at 9:30 every night, and he does not want it micro-waved.

The girls in the class verbally attacked him. They told him he was inconsiderate of his mother, that he was a male chauvinist, and that he was insensitive.

Abby erred in agreeing with them, a transgression she suspected but later understood when she realized how different his culture is from hers.

Through her experiences, Abby learned that teachers can further validate students by being sensitive to their backgrounds and cultures, by recognizing the importance of their individual perspectives, by validating feelings and encouraging connections, and by accepting each student as important in his or her own right.

One evening, while the class was working quietly, Keon asked aloud, "Miss, if I gave you $500,000, would you quit teaching?"

Abby responded immediately with a resounding "Yes."

He looked disappointed. He was silent. She thought that he had hoped she wasn't able to be "bought out." Abby believed she had let him down.

A few minutes later she teasingly asked, "Keon, if I gave you $500,000, would you go straight?" He smiled his sweetest smile and said, "Ah, I'd like to have something 'legit,' Miss, but I'll always have something on the side. Keeps life exciting."

Where does a teacher go from here? She can't give him the desire to stay out of trouble. His father has been in jail since he was a young boy, so that potential role model doesn't exist for him.

In Keon, Abby sees kindness and sensitivity. She sees a genuinely nice person: respectful, bright, a leader, charismatic, fun. On the negative side, she would say he is not reliable or dependable and perhaps not always trustworthy. Yet, overall, he has so much potential. In jail he has no potential, and in that setting all of his assets turn to liabilities.

Keon is aware of his strengths. He is a ladies man--very flirtatious and perhaps lacking sincerity in those moments. Whatever path he chooses, he just has to keep in mind that he has choices, all of which have consequences--good or bad.

LESSON LEARNED: BE SENSITIVE. As mentioned under "Show Respect to Get Respect," having someone pat my head in the middle of class seemed inappropriate. However, under the circumstance with this student, it was appropriate; it was just unexpected.

Being put on the spot by an unexpected question taught Abby a lesson, i.e., "I must think before I speak."

Teachers have to be sensitive to the fact that the person they are working with does not have the same background and experiences that they have had in life, therefore, they cannot expect them to react in a similar manner.

Abby learned that showing respect, being nonjudgmental and accepting, providing a safe atmosphere and seeking their strengths are very important actions, but showing sensitivity is the ultimate compliment to an individual.

Human Nature Law #9:
SET BOUNDARIES

The home and street experiences of most high school dropouts are responsible for many of the survival characteristics this population has adopted to "get by" in life. Some students have a difficult time learning that there are times when they do have to follow the rules; and if they choose not to, then they receive the consequences. A perfect example of this is the following young lady's story.

Julia is cute, lively, and certainly outgoing--traits which would appear, and which Abby originally believed, would make her an asset to the class. She volunteers to read aloud. She answers questions when asked. She brings enthusiasm to the class. These are the delightful aspects of Julia.

She is also a chatterbox with her best friend, as many her age are. The first day of class, after asking the girls numerous times to stop talking, Abby just separated them--problem solved, or so she thought.

The problem with Julia in class is not her talking; it's her belief that she does not have to follow any rules but her own. She will talk to her friend across people while the teacher is teaching, if she so desires.

During a test, where she was allowed to work with the person next to her, she turned around and gave answers to the boys at the table behind her, because she wanted to. Abby asked her not to work with anyone but her assigned partner.

She continued the same exact behavior in spite of being asked three times not to talk because this is a test. She finally complied, turned around to her desk, and then called out the answer to the test question so all of the class could hear. Is that acceptable behavior in an adult school? She was asked to leave.

On her way out, Julia uttered, "If you think my attitude will be better on Monday, you are in for a big surprise." Is that a threat?

When Abby returned the following week, Julia showed up for class. Abby took her into the hall to talk to her. She asked her to explain why she had acted as she did during the test, and Julia explained that the boys behind her asked her for the answer. Abby asked her why she called out the answer, and she said, "Oh, did everyone hear me?" She knew they had, especially when, for fairness, Abby repeated it for the few who were not paying attention.

Abby told her she felt that she was an asset to the class, that she has more personality than three people and that Abby genuinely enjoyed her as a student; but Abby could not put up with that behavior. She told Julia she would have to follow the rules if she wants to be in this class.

Julia appeared contrite and agreed to follow the rules, so Abby relented and allowed her back into the classroom. Abby reminded her that she was on thin ice and the next infraction would cost her her seat in class, for which there is a waiting list. She seemed to understand.

Three days later, and Abby's first time in front of the class again, although only to take roll, Julia again is sitting with her friend, talking. Abby reminded them they could not ever sit together. They pushed their chairs apart so another person could have moved in the space, although no one did.

Miss Jackson, the student teacher in training, taught the class, while Abby worked in the back of the class, then the side of the room. As Miss Jackson was teaching, Abby was distracted from her work by chattering. Guess who?

Julia and her friend had pushed their chairs back together again and were talking like magpies, totally ignoring the teacher. As they continued talking, Abby couldn't say anything because of the teaching going on in front of the room. When Miss Jackson paused, Abby jumped in and asked Julia to see her.

With anger, Julia approached Abby. Abby reminded her that she had asked at the beginning of class that she and her friend were not to sit together, and Abby reminded her of their agreement for her being back in class.

Rather than apologize or take responsibility for her action, Julia proceeded to tell Abby that she was out of line for speaking to her regarding her actions in this class because she was not the teacher of this class. She was not in charge; and if Miss Jackson didn't like what she was doing, it was up to Miss Jackson to tell her, because it was her class, not Abby's.

At this point, Abby found listening to her defiance and arrogance to be a bit much, so she calmly interjected, "And you are no longer a part of this class and may leave." She left, announcing to the class in anger that she had been kicked out.

This young lady has so many wonderful attributes going for her, all of which will count for little if she continues with her belief that she does not have to follow the rules or be sensitive to other people. She obviously cannot tolerate not having her own way. To her, the only rules she has to follow are those of her own making or liking. She believes she is "entitled" to act however she pleases.

Part of the growing/maturing process, as Abby sees it, is learning how to interact with others, how to play the game. Abby would have failed to do her job had she allowed Julia to maintain and act out on that belief in Abby's class. Someone has to say "no" to this young lady. If every student believes and acts as she does, there would be pandemonium in the classroom.

Abby sees her as a spoiled child who has tantrums if she does not get her way. Abby hopes she recognizes that limits are there for a reason, and sometimes she just has to adjust. She hasn't learned that yet.

Abby believes that if a student is not cooperative, have the principal switch this child to another classroom. If the second teacher has the same experience, the student should be dismissed. Boundaries do have to be set.

LESSON LEARNED: SET BOUNDARIES. If everyone in society did what they wanted to do, when they wanted to do it, the world would be in chaos. Small children find life easier when boundaries are set, in spite of their protests. Students have to recognize and follow the rules and regulations of society in order to succeed.

Abby also learned that being "right" does not always work, as illustrated in
the following ditty:

> "Here lies the body of William Jay,
> Who died maintaining his right of way.
> He was right, dead right, as he sped along,
> But he is just as dead as if he were wrong."

Human Nature Law #10:
HAVE FUN/FEEL GOOD

Abby believes that almost anything can be made fun. She recalls the stories she has read regarding the famous Pike Place Fish Market in Seattle, Washington, where the employees throw the fish to one another, sing, laugh, and have a ball--selling fish! What a delightful place to work!

According to Abby, teaching should be a pleasurable experience. She wants kids to enjoy the lesson, find the humor, and have a good time. Human nature seeks pleasure and avoids pain. Sometimes school can feel "painful."

Specifically, one of the least favorite lessons Abby had to teach to high school students each week was vocabulary. That is, it was unpopular until she divided the students into groups, assigned each group 5 words and had them come up with a skit with only 15 minutes preparation time.

Vocabulary day came to be one of the most enjoyable days of the week. The skits were creative and fun—sometimes belly-laugh fun, and the test scores went up on average by 10 points in every class.

"Having fun" means "feeling good." Abby's question is always, "How can we make our lives better than they are now?" Or better yet, "How can we make our students' lives better than they are now?"

Abby hopes that some of the tips in the following paragraph will help everyone live a happier life, especially in dealing with other people.

To begin with, Abby believes there are three things each of us needs for ourselves. We need food—wholesome and nutritious—to nourish our bodies. We need shelter—a safe place to live. We need validation—someone to let us know we are important to the world. When we have these three essentials—food, shelter, and validation—in our lives, we can work on being the best that we can be

Abby suggested that

TO HAVE FUN, LIVE THE BEST LIFE YOU CAN
BY BEING THE BEST THAT YOU CAN BE

To feel GOOD, choose and experience
any of these "feel-good" emotions:
Passion
Bliss
Happiness
Reverence
Joy
Trust
Optimism
Inspiration
Harmony
Appreciation

Abby recommends that most importantly, every day, we express GRATI-TUDE and seek BEAUTY, validate people, look for their positives, and show everyone kindness, appreciation, and respect.

Thoughts are choices and can be positive or negative. It is up to the individual to make the selection!

A recent *Washington Post* article chronicles the importance of laughter in the lives of Carl Reiner, Mel Brooks, Betty White, Norman Lear, and Dick Van-Dyke, all comedians in their 90's. Carl Reiner, 97, believes humor has enriched his life and boosted his longevity.

One commonality everyone shares is the enjoyment of laughter. It makes you feel good. It relieves tension. Studies suggest that laughter can improve health and possibly stave off disease, thereby extending life. It also eases stress and helps the ill cope with their sickness and pain.

"A friendly sense of humor will bless you with better social relations as well as coping skills, and the reduced risk of dying early," says Sven Svebak, professor emeritus at the Norwegian University of Science and Technology, who has studied the health impact of humor for more than 50 years. "A friendly sense of humor acts like shock absorbers in a car a mental shock absorber in everyday life to help us cope better with a range of frustrations, hassles, and irritations."

Laughter and humor are great prescriptions for these high school dropouts who suffer from their own range of frustrations, hassles and irritations.

Another recommendation for humor comes from Edward Creagan, professor of medical oncology at the Mayo Clinic College of Medicine and Science. He says, "When people are funny, they attract other people, and community connectedness is the social currency for longevity."

A great motto for everyone to adopt is "Live, Laugh, Love, and Learn!"

On the other hand,
To feel BAD, choose
Judgment and/or negativity through feelings of
Revenge
Excuses
Procrastination
Anger
Justification
Gossip
Hate
Ill Will
Blame
Sickness
Gloom
Despair
Criticism
Hatred
Restrictions
Anxiety
Fear
Shame

These feelings equal depression, sadness, "I don't feel good."

Abby believes that if everyone's ultimate goal is to feel good, what better way than to have fun while working to become a better person and helping someone else also become a better person!

LESSON LEARNED: HAVE FUN/FEEL GOOD! Enjoy!

Human Nature Law #11:
SMILE: It warms a room.

Abby's recommendations:

People gravitate toward a smile. It is welcoming. It is validating.

Become aware of how, when you smile, you automatically feel better. When you are smiling, it is hard to feel sad or angry.

Make it a point to smile and laugh every single day. It feels good and is good for you mentally and physically.

"A smile is happiness you'll find right under your nose." - Tom Wilson

Human Nature Law #12:
BE (OR ACT) ENTHUSIASTIC about everything you do.

More of Abby's recommendations:

Enthusiasm is contagious; it carries over to your students.

Some of the well-known people who have spoken about enthusiasm are as follows:

• Act enthusiastic and you'll be enthusiastic. - Dale Carnegie

• Mark Twain said he was born excited and that is the reason for his success.

• Napoleon Hill: Enthusiasm guarantees your point will be positive.

• Thomas Edison: When a man dies, if he has passed enthusiasm along to his children, he has left them an estate of incalculable value.

• Emerson: Nothing great was ever achieved without enthusiasm.

• Years wrinkle the skin; lack of enthusiasm wrinkles the soul.

• Maxwell Maltz: You must create [enthusiasm] yourself without waiting for someone to thrust it upon you. Enthusiasm is a thought turned into a performance; it is the kinetic energy that propels you to your destination. Enthusiasm implies that you believe in yourself, that you concentrate with courage, that you practice self-discipline, that you have a dream, that you see victory in the distance.

Human Nature Law #13
Remember, **PEOPLE HAVE TWO BASIC NEEDS:
TO KNOW THEY ARE LOVABLE AND TO KNOW THEY ARE
WORTHWHILE.**

SUMMARY OF HUMAN NATURE LAWS

Human Nature Law #1: SHOW RESPECT TO GET RESPECT

Human Nature Law #2: **BE NONJUDGMENTAL**

Human Nature Law #3: SEEK THE STRENGTHS OF EVERY STUDENT

Human Nature Law #4: PROVIDE A SAFE ATMOSPHERE

Human Nature Law #5: KNOW THAT YOU CANNOT <u>NOT</u> COMMUNICATE

Human Nature Law #6: **SET HIGH EXPECTATIONS**

Human Nature Law #7: MAKE SINCERITY YOUR #1 PRIORITY

Human Nature Law #8: **BE SENSITIVE**

Human Nature Law #9: **SET BOUNDARIES**

Human Nature Law #10: **HAVE FUN**

Human Nature Law #11: **SMILE:** It warms a room.

Human Nature Law #12: **BE (OR ACT) ENTHUSIASTIC** about everything you do.

Human Nature Law #13: Remember, PEOPLE HAVE TWO BASIC NEEDS: TO KNOW THEY ARE LOVABLE AND TO KNOW THEY ARE WORTHWHILE.

If these laws are the accepted commonalities amongst most people, how can they be effectively implemented?

CHAPTER THREE
IMPLEMENTATION

Abby is well aware of the ineffectiveness of "telling" people to be kind or enthusiastic or nonjudgmental or any of the Human Nature Laws.

She is well aware that if a student doesn't feel she is worthwhile or lovable, she may find it difficult to be kind to others, especially those who have been unkind to her. He might be challenged to be enthusiastic. That's human nature.

The change has to come from within, not from being "told" how to act, but to experience the desire to accept and act on the Laws of Human Nature.

What is important to kids? And to all people?

If the goal is to have every child believe in him or herself, whose validation is most important to them? Abby thought about that and remembered a story she had read many years ago that impacted her at the time and is timeless and significant even today.

That memory motivated Abby to develop the first course, a program where every student will be validated by their peers every time they speak. That course is called **"Speaking for Teens."**

The second course is about them. When Abby started teaching at VoTech, she had written a book on teaching English to disinterested students. It bombed. The next week, she brought in copies of the Manual for a book she had written years ago, ***Discover Your Passion***. It was an immediate hit! Why? Because it was about them. The exercises recognized what is special about each person, so Abby taught English through ***Discover Your Passion For Teens***.

Because of her concern about high school dropouts, Abby had developed a program called *Kids Mentoring Kids*. Upper grades students mentor lower grade students. Read more about that in the next section.

That is what the following three programs do.

1. They provide the experience of helping younger students who look up to them as a result.

2. They learn the basic human relation skills through teaching them to underclassmen.

3. They learn the importance of listening, a skill that extends far beyond the classroom.

4. They experience the problems of others and through helping them, are able to solve many of their own problems.

CHAPTER FOUR
COURSE #1 - SPEAKING FOR TEENS

After Abby was satisfied with her Laws of Human Nature as applied to students, she thought long and hard about how to implement the concepts in a realistic and enjoyable manner. The first major challenges Abby confronted were timing and "buy-in" from students and the administration. How could she convince teachers and administrators that self-esteem, communication skills, and human relation skills are worth spending time on where there is no way to empirically measure their progress?

Abby believes that every child should be exposed to ways to maximize their skills and abilities. What vehicle could she develop that would teach and demonstrate respect for one another and be recognized as something of value by school administrators?

She started with one course that she considered to be a no-fail course, a course that would assure acceptance among a diverse group of kids, engender a belief in oneself, and would be an opportunity to experience all 13 Human Nature Laws.

With 180 days of school a year, divided into 36 weeks or 18 weeks a semester, Abby designed her first course, a 14-course (allowing a couple of weeks of leeway time including vacations and holidays) that would enable students to find the best in their peers while learning a skill and putting all 13 Human Nature Laws into practice.

As mentioned previously, Abby was motivated to develop a course that incorporated acceptance and validation on a daily basis. She made her decision after reading the touching story of teacher in Minnesota who wrote about an unforgettable elementary student, Mark Eklund, a likable but frustrating student because of his inability to stay quiet in class. This is his teacher's story about Mark.

He was in the first third grade class I taught at Saint Mary's School in Morris, Minn. All 34 of my students were dear to me, but Mark Eklund was one in a million. Very neat in appearance but had that happy-to-be-alive attitude that made even his occasional mischievousness delightful.

Mark talked incessantly. I had to remind him again and again that talking without permission was not acceptable. What impressed me so much, though, was his sincere response every time I had to correct him for misbehaving – "Thank you for correcting me, Sister!" I didn't know what to make of it at first, but before long I became accustomed to hearing it many times a day.

One morning my patience was growing thin when Mark talked once too often, and then I made a novice teacher's mistake. I looked at Mark and said, "If you say one more word, I am going to tape your mouth shut!"

It wasn't ten seconds later when Chuck blurted out, "Mark is talking again." I hadn't asked any of the students to help me watch Mark, but since I had stated the punishment in front of the class, I had to act on it. I remember the scene as if it had occurred this morning.

I walked to my desk, very deliberately opened my drawer and took out a roll of masking tape. Without saying a word, I proceeded to Mark's desk, tore off two pieces of tape and made a big X with them over his mouth. I then returned to the front of the room. As I glanced at Mark to see how he was doing, he winked at me. That did it! I started laughing. The class cheered as I walked back to Mark's desk, removed the tape, and shrugged my shoulders. His first words were, "Thank you for correcting me, Sister."

At the end of the year, I was asked to teach junior-high math. The years flew by, and before I knew it Mark was in my classroom again. He was more handsome than ever and just as polite. Since he had to listen carefully to my instruction in the "new math," he did not talk as much in ninth grade as he had in third.

One Friday, things just didn't feel right. We had worked hard on a new concept all week, and I sensed that the students were frowning, frustrated with themselves and edgy with one another. I had to stop this crankiness before it got out of hand. So, I asked them to list the names of the other students in the room on two sheets of paper, leaving a space between each name. Then I told them to think of the nicest thing they could say about each of their classmates and write it down. It took the remainder of the class period to finish their assignment, and as the students left the room, each one handed me the papers. Charlie smiled. Mark said, "Thank you for teaching me, Sister. Have a good weekend." That Saturday I wrote down the name of each student on a separate sheet of paper, and I listed what everyone else had said about that individual.

On Monday I gave each student his or her list. Before long, the entire class was smiling. "Really?" I heard whispered. "I never knew that meant anything to anyone!" "I didn't know others liked me so much."

No one ever mentioned those papers in class again. I never knew if they discussed them after class or with their parents, but it didn't matter. The exercise had accomplished its purpose. The students were happy with themselves and one another again.

That group of students moved on. Several years later, after I returned from vacation, my parents met me at the airport. As we were driving home, Mother asked me the usual
questions about the trip, the weather, my experiences in general. There was a lull in the conversation. Mother gave Dad a sideways glance and simply says, "Dad?" My father cleared his throat as he usually did before something important. "The Eklunds called last night," he began "Really?" I said. "I haven't heard from them in years. I wonder how Mark is." Dad responded quietly. "Mark was killed in Vietnam," he said. "The funeral is tomorrow, and his parents would like it if you could attend." To this day I can still point to the exact spot on I-494 where Dad told me about Mark.

I had never seen a serviceman in a military coffin before. Mark looked so handsome, so mature. All I could think at that moment was, "Mark, I would give all the masking tape in the world if only you would talk to me."

The church was packed with Mark's friends. Chuck's sister sang "The Battle

Hymn of the Republic." Why did it have to rain on the day of the funeral? It was difficult enough at the graveside. The pastor said the usual prayers, and the bugler played taps.

One by one those who loved Mark took a last walk by the coffin and sprinkled it with holy water. I was the last one to bless the coffin. As I stood there, one of the soldiers who acted as pallbearer came up to me. "Were you Mark's math teacher?" He asked. I nodded as I continued to stare at the coffin. "Mark talked about you a lot." He said.

After the funeral, most of Mark's former classmates headed to Chuck's farmhouse for lunch. Mark's mother and father were there, obviously waiting for me. "We want to show you something, his father said, taking a wallet out of his pocket. "They found this on Mark when he was killed. We thought you might recognize it."

Opening the billfold, he carefully removed two worn pieces of notebook paper that had obviously been taped, folded and refolded many times. I knew without looking that the papers were the ones on which I had listed all the good things each of Mark's classmates had said about him.

"Thank you so much for doing that," Mark's mother said. "As you can see, Mark treasured it." Mark's classmates started to gather around us. Charlie smiled rather sheepishly and said, "I still have my list. I keep it in the top drawer of my desk at home." Chuck's wife said, "Chuck asked me to put his in our wedding album." "I have mine too," Marilyn said. "It's in my diary." Then Vicky, another classmate, reached into her pocketbook, took out her wallet and showed her worn and frazzled list to the group. "I carry this with me at all times," Vicki said without batting an eyelash. "I think we all saved our lists."

That's when I finally sat down and cried. I cried for Mark and for all his friends who would never see him again.

The density of people in society is so thick that we forget that life will end one day. And we don't know when that one day will be. So please, tell the people you love and care for, that they are special and important. Tell them, before it is too late.

Although Abby had read this story many years ago, it always stayed in her mind. Mark's teacher had implemented a simple act of acceptance and validation wrapped up in a list, a list that impacted each individual in the class. Abby pondered on how to replicate this in a meaningful, relevant, fun manner.

After many months of work, Abby produced her 14-week course called **"Speaking for Teens."** In addition to learning speaking skills—openings, evidence, closings, body language, and attitude training, Abby added a "list-type" of activity.

Every student had a card with his or her name at the top and an assigned number (it's easier to find numbers than alphabetized names). If there are 25 students in the class, each student writes his or her name on 25 cards along with the number. The cards are then dispersed among the other students, so every member has a complete packet to cards for every other classmate.

On the wall is a chart listing three areas students are to comment on after each person speaks: the talk itself, the delivery of the talk, the audience reaction to the talk. The one caveat is **ONLY POSITIVES** can be written on the cards—absolutely no negative comments.

As each student goes to the front of the room, he/she gives the teacher a sheet of paper with the first line and the last line of the talk. After the talk, the teacher asks for two comments from class members, again, only positives.

The teacher adds one more positive, then on the student's paper, writes 1) a positive comment, 2) an area of improvement comment, and 3) another positive statement. The students' grades are dependent on how well they address the "area of improvement" comment.

The impact of this course proved to be the most satisfying of Abby's entire career. She has over 19 pages of testimonials from kids who used their experience in the class when applying to college or for a job. A brief sampling includes: (The entire 19 pages can be found at https://bit.ly/2Mkflgc)

CONFIDENCE

• Michael J: First speech: "I was sweating and shaking. I was nervous to get in front of the class. I then felt better when my classmates clapped for me when I was going up. I felt a little better, but I was still nervous. When I finished my talk my classmates clapped for me and said I did a good job. I also felt better because they were quiet, and they listened to my talk."

Daniel B: "I gained more confidence when talking in front of an audience."

• Carlo E: "Then I present a show of my own, hear positive comments from my classmates and feel good about myself. I still don't want to be a center of attention but now I'm more comfortable doing what I have to do."

• Vera M: "Public Speaking is the best class I have ever taken. I saw the change in people like C and S who were never outspoken and the change in them is incredible. I learned more about my image."

• Kate K: "I feel I have gotten a lot out of this course. I am confident when speaking in front of a group of people (especially my peers). I know I can get through an interview successfully. In saying all this, it comes as an obvious statement when I say I thoroughly enjoyed this course."

• Tina C: "As a result of this course, I have gained a confidence before my audience that I have never felt before."

• Jessica F: "I have learned a lot from it because my confidence has grown and now I can't wait to give my next speech."

• Diane S: "This class has made a big difference in my life. Before Effective Speaking I was a lot shyer than I am now, a couple of months later. The first time I went to make a talk, I was scared to death. I was worried about what the rest of the class would think. Now I feel so comfortable talking in front of people. I actually have a lot more fun giving the talks now that I have overcome my fear."

Other areas of improvement as a result of the course include Self-Esteem, Understanding of Others, Friendship, Acceptance, Nervousness, and Miscellaneous for a total of 19 pages. To read them all, go to https://bit.ly/2Mkflgc.

Abby was pleased with the results of the **Speaking for Teens** course, a one-semester elective. She believed the next important aspect of a high school student's training should be in the area of finding their passion or purpose in life. See **Discover Your Passion for Kids** next.

CHAPTER FIVE
COURSE #2: "Discover Your Passion for Teens"

In the **Speaking for Teens** course, the Laws of Human Nature were addressed. The second part of what Abby determined to be needed for high school students is direction. This course is an 8-week elective, preferably for juniors. Every student is special, and this course zeros in on what makes each one special and how that knowledge can help them plan their futures.

Computerized aptitude tests are frequently used to determine careers in which students may be successful. *Discover Your Passion* takes a different approach. On a computerized test, a student must choose one answer, e.g. your favorite color. If their favorite color isn't listed, the test is skewed, albeit ever so slightly.

With the exercises in *Discover Your Passion,* students are asked questions they can discuss with their peers, and there are never any wrong answers. These sessions are opportunities for insightful thinking for each student taking this elective.

Abby pondered a number of questions unrelated to her academic schedule. She thought, "Wouldn't it be nice if everyone could do what they wanted to do every day and still earn money? How great would it be to feel excited when you awaken every morning? Wouldn't everyone like to feel that what they do makes a difference in the world?"

Abby believes all of this is possible once a person knows what their passion is and knows how to put that passion to work. Master motivator and author, Barbara Sher, says it best in the title of her book, *I Would Do What I Love If Only I Knew What It Was.*

By the last session of this elective, Abby's experience is that students will know not only what their passion is but also how to earn money pursuing that passion whether it is full-time or as an income- producing hobby.

Abby recognizes that no two people are alike. Everyone has unique talents, knowledge, skills, and abilities. Finding which skill, which bit of knowledge, or which talent a person most enjoys using will lead to discovering their passion.

Two of Abby's favorite people concur. Wayne Dyer says, "There is no scarcity of opportunity to make a living at what you love; there's only a scarcity of resolve to make it happen. Even Oprah says, "Your job is to discover what your true calling is." Therein lies your happiness.

Abby developed *Discover Your Passion* as a course to help students discover their passion and earn money doing what they love. The four major objectives of this program are
to help them clarify their passion,
to prepare them for a job search or help some of the students to find their business,
to familiarize them with marketing basics, and
to help them learn how to make their dreams come true. Students can progress at their own rate or work in small groups.

She created major lesson divisions according to the information regarding the topic. Some sessions will take longer than others. Her experience is that students enjoy the journey, whether they are headed to college or to a vocational school to master a skill or to go out and find a job.

Abby designed the program to allow each participant to recognize what is special about themselves and to find a direction in life. The information students glean from their responses are important pieces necessary to complete their jigsaw passion puzzle. Fit them all together and they will have their passion.

THE IMPORTANCE OF HAVING A PURPOSE

Another book that impacted Abby is *Man's Search for Meaning,* where Victor Frankl tells of his horror-filled days as a prisoner in a Nazi prison camp. He said he made an interesting observation about those people who survived the terror and hardships of their ordeals.

He stated, in effect, that those who had a purpose in life survived; those who did not see any hope or believe they a purpose, died, even if physiologically equal. That is a significant observation.

Similarly, Wayne Dyer in *Real Magic* recalls the words of the prison inmate, "Nothing is more likely to help a person overcome or endure troubles than the consciousness of having a task in life."

Alter his words a bit by using the word passion in place of task, Abby read "Nothing is more likely to help a person overcome or endure troubles than the consciousness of having a passion in life." She believes that that is what teachers want students to uncover as they progress through this course.

The #1 deadly fear of many people is having lived a meaningless life. Abby's husband started his own business many years ago, because, as he said, he didn't want to wake up on his deathbed and say to himself, "I should have given it a shot."

"The only courage you ever need is the courage to live your heart's desire." -Oprah

Now is the time!!! This elective is the way!!!

In her e-zine, Barbara Sher, author of *Wishcraft*, wrote "You're all obligated to do what you love because that's where your gifts lie and those gifts belong to all of us."

Implicit in that statement are **three premises**:
1) everyone is here for a purpose, and
2) everyone is here to help others, and
3) gravitating toward pleasure, e.g., doing what you love, is not only okay, it is mandatory if you want to help others and if you are seeking the wonderful illusives called happiness, satisfaction, and serenity.

That reminds Abby of her favorite quote "The time to be happy is now; the place to be happy is here, and the way to be happy is by helping others." -

Charles Englehardt. That says it all.

Abby strongly believes that now that they are in high school, the time has come for students to discover how to use their gifts to make the world a better place. She believes that doing so will not only enrich their lives but also the lives of others. This is an opportunity to make the world a better place.

Having defined the baker's dozen of essential human nature laws, Abby got busy working on ways to implement what she felt was important to work on in order to motivate kids to learn and to be their best selves. She knew she couldn't just tell others to show respect to get respect, be non-judgmental, etc. **She needed a way for kids to experience these laws and hopefully adopt them.**

Over the next few years, Abby worked on the development of these three separate courses that would show rather than tell the laws of human nature with the intent of having them "buy in."

She started with Mindset or Belief and integrated the concepts into the three courses but devoted one course, **"Discover Your Passion for Teens,"** as the opportunity for teens to study themselves without judgment and make decisions based on what they experienced in the course.

The importance of belief! Napoleon Hill wrote in his book *Think and Grow Rich*: "What the mind can see and believe, it can achieve."

Abby believes the concept is still the same; it's still true -- if a student's mind can think up or conceive of an idea **and** believe in it, he can achieve it.

Abby continues: "If you believe you can do something, what's stopping you? What have you gotten to believe that acts as an obstacle to your success? Do you believe you can't "get" math, you can't make friends, you aren't bright, you can't sing, you are clumsy, etc." Some may be true, and that's fine. The point is, if you believe it, you act accordingly.

Abby recognizes that a person might **want** to be a singer, but if they can't carry a tune, they're not going to believe they can be a singer. Maybe they're horrible in math. If so, they're probably not going to WANT to be a scientist or an engineer, but they may be great in something else.

"If your mind can conceive and believe in doing something, you can achieve it. If you believe you can, what's stopping you? What have you gotten to believe that acts as an obstacle to your success?"

One of Abby's favorite sayings is from Henry Ford, the founder of Ford motors and the first assembly line for the manufacture of cars. He said, **"If you think you can or you think you can't, you're right."** "If you think you can or if you think you can't, you're right."

To prove her point, Abby continued, "Belief applies not only to human beings, but also to the animal kingdom, even insects.

EXAMPLE # 1: If you catch flees and put them in a jar, they will jump up and hit their heads, jump up and hit their heads on the lid until finally they believe they can't get out. So, they sit on the bottom of the jar.

You can take the lid off of the jar, you can move the jar around, upside down, and the flees will not jump again. Why? Because they believe they can't get out. The point is: the flea comes to believe he cannot escape, even when the route to escape is clear; therefore, in his head, he cannot escape. That's how strong belief is.

EXAMPLE #2: Now, from a much larger point of view is that of an elephant. You may see a little elephant tied with a thin chain that goes around the elephant's leg attached to a stake in the ground, and well the elephant gets bigger and bigger and bigger, and finally there is this huge pachyderm who is tied to a stake in the ground with a little, thin chain. Obviously, he could just move it, pull his foot up, take it away; but he doesn't because—he believes he can't. He won't do what he can't believe he can do. This is the power of belief.

Like the elephants, many of us, especially kids, go through life hanging onto a belief that we cannot do something, simply because we failed at it once before.

EXAMPLE #3: Another example is Dr. Herbert Benson, a researcher from Harvard University. He was involved with a meditation movement way back when transcendental meditation became popular. Benson spent his career studying, among other things, meditation and the mind. He traveled to Tibet and observed how the mind can be trained as evidenced by the spiritual men and the monks could sit on a mountain top dressed in only a loincloth covered with a sheet and have the snow melt that fell onto the sheet.

From years of intense prayer and solitude, these monks were mentally capable of raising their body temperatures.

In some tribes, Dr. Benson found that the shaman or the medicine man could point to somebody after a trial and say, "Go home and die," and the person went home and died because he believed so strongly in the shaman—again, the power of belief!

If you think you can or you think you can't, you're right.

Frequently kids, especially "at risk" kids believe they're incapable in some manner, who believe they're not accepted, who believe the teachers are being unfair to them. Some of their beliefs might be true, but they must be listened to and encouraged."

The point is," according to Abby, "our beliefs determine our success or lack of success in life. Kids need to know they are worthwhile, that they have something to offer the world. Everybody does, but sometimes talent is just not utilized because a person doesn't believe in the existence of that talent.

Our beliefs guide us as it does our students.

ANOTHER EXAMPLE OF BELIEFS: Sometimes beliefs have a tremendous effect on a person of any age. For two summers Abby had taught school administrators in Lithuania. This country had been under Russian rule for 50 years and had been subjected to a lot of destruction, including their educational system, especially where their schools were concerned. An American organization, A.P.P.L.E. (American Professional Partnership for Lithuanian Education) was founded and worked with teachers for 25 years before disbanding. American instructors worked with school teachers and administrators to teach them the latest ways that Americans do things in order to try to help them get their education system up to par.

They teachers had some beliefs that are different than what Abby was used to.

In the classrooms, there was no air-conditioning. On one hot day, Abby opened a window and opened the door to get a cross breeze. Immediately, one of the ladies immediately got up and closed the window or closed the door. Abby then reopened the window and reopened the door, and they would say with fear in their voices, "No, no, you can't do that because if you sit in a draft, you'll get a cold and possibly die."

They believed what they said! They believed if they sat in a draft, they would die. Abby could not deny their wishes.

When Abby first got married, her mother-in-law was horrified that she washed my hair at night and went to bed. She believed Abby would die. She would get a cold and die. She believed that.

What beliefs do you, the reader, have about yourself, about your background? Are they positive or negative?

Abby always thought she couldn't go to college because "a nice Irish girl didn't run away from home" and "You're too big for your britches." That's what her father told her, but Abby changed her belief and started to believe she could go to college and pay for it herself, and she did.

What about your abilities? Do you believe you're good in math? Do you believe you're good in English? Do you believe you're good in science? Do you believe you're good in phys. ed.? Can you sing? Can you dance? What are your beliefs about yourself physically, mentally, spiritually? Those beliefs determine how you do in life.

And, of course, Abby believes the easy answer is: all you have to do is change those negative beliefs or have somebody point out to you what your strengths are. It's amazing when somebody hits the nail right on the head. You know it; they know it.

Every person has strengths and weaknesses. In this course, **Discover Your Passion for Teens,** Abby has exercises that enable each student to find theirs; and, along the way, may find their life's work. There are no wrong answers!

CHAPTER SIX
COURSE #3: "Kids Mentoring Kids"

Abby was still concerned about the number of dropouts, mentally and/or physically, in the schools, especially schools in tougher areas.

Having taught in one capacity or another for decades, she finds her heart goes out to those kids who "fall between the cracks," the potential dropouts. It is for that reason that Abby developed the two programs already mentioned, both of which are enriching and fun. They are validating of each participant; they provide direction, and they teach communication skills, including human relations skills which translates immediately to improved civility among classmates.

Finally, it came to her: why not use the remaining quarter of the year, as an elective, to train kids to mentor other kids—juniors mentoring incoming freshmen.

Abby's experience proved how one high school club (taught in 1/2 of one semester) and two electives can keep potential dropouts in school.

As a result, Abby developed **Kids Mentoring Kids**, an elective for all juniors. She also developed a program which shows:

How to set up a high school club that will provide acceptance, validation, and guidance to every child
How to train club participants in listening skills and human relation skills
How to improve college acceptance rates through participation in this club
How to help every student discover their passion or purpose in life through a one-semester elective
How to practice interviewing skills through this same elective
How to improve speaking skills, self-confidence and esteem through a second one-semester elective.

A *Star Ledger* Editorial headline read: **Cause of death: Gangs!!!** "A study has found that more than half of all homicides in New Jersey are related to gang activity. . ."

Further in the editorial: "Law enforcement is only part of the solution. The best way to protect against the resulting violence is to understand the reasons young people are drawn to gangs . . . to find ways to counter that attraction." Abby believes that an ideal "way to counter that attraction" is to start using mentoring in the high schools--juniors and seniors mentoring freshmen and sophomores or in lower grades where 8th graders mentor 4th graders. A club similar to the Key Club or Spanish Club or Poetry Club in high schools could be set up for the upper-class students where they would have an opportunity to not only discuss their underclass student challenges with the group but also master the basics of human nature and mentoring ethics that they can apply to all parts of their lives.

If every child were mentored as a freshman and then became a mentor, the world would indeed be a better place in which to live. Civility would be main-stream.

An administration complaint could be lack of time. It takes time to set up the appointment, get to the appointment, go there, return, etc. With this pro-gram, however, mentoring could be a part of the curriculum.

Abby found the mentoring experience to be a definite **win-win** situation. The person being mentored knows someone cares, someone is always there for them, merely a classroom or a phone call away, and someone can offer advice and guidance, someone older and wiser, even if it is only a couple of years.

On the other side of the coin, mentors have an opportunity to practice their listening skills and their human relation skills. They have an opportunity to be responsible for another person, which in turn makes them grow and be-come more self-sufficient.

The responsibility of having someone to mentor is something that cannot be taught; it can only be experienced.

What Abby learned from her diverse teaching opportunities is simple: Everyone is special in some way, and when a person is able to recognize and act on that something special, that person and the world benefits.

One of the best ways for high school kids to find what is special about themselves is to become a mentor. Abby developed this training to allow mentors to learn and know the tools to use to find what's special in others; however, it is the practice of using the tools with underclassmen that allows the significance of the tools to be internalized by the mentor.

They learn by doing. By putting their knowledge into practice while mentoring underclassmen, they "get" it!!

Abby believes that the secret of success for almost every person is to have someone in your corner (parent, friend, relative, priest, minister, teacher), rooting them on, cheering for them, helping them, validating them, and at times pointing out more effective ways to handle people and situations in life without tearing them down in the process.

IMPRESSIVE STATISTICS:
• A research study provided these results on mentoring. "Children who met with a mentor three times a month for one year were 46 percent less likely to begin using illegal drugs, 27 percent decrease in initiating alcohol use, 37 percent decrease in lying to parents, 52 percent less likely to skip school, and 33 percent less likely to get into fights." (Statistics from a nationwide review of Big Brother/Big Sister's Programs by Tierney & Grossman)

• Why has mentoring grown into a social movement supported by government, schools, businesses and religious institutions alike? Because it works.

• Recognize that a mentor is a caring and concerned person. A mentor is a listener and a guide.

The value of mentoring is immeasurable! Take a look at the **STATISTICS,** keeping in mind that a large percentage of inmates are high school dropouts.

• Over 70,000 people will be released from state prison in New Jersey over the next five years. Check the number leaving your state's prisons.

• The average yearly cost of housing an inmate in New Jersey is $50,000. What is it in your state?

• The recidivism rate is over 60%. Two thirds of all prison releases end up back behind bars within three years.

• In 2004, a third of the 14,000 inmates who left state prison were let go with no obligation to hold a job, submit to drug tests or report to a parole officer.

• States spend an estimated $44 billion annually on prisons alone, not including the costs of arrest and prosecution, the damage to crime victims, or the impact on families and communities.

• A high percentage of dropouts end up in prison, costing the state approximately $50,000 a year per inmate. If 8 out of 10 potential dropouts stayed out of prison as a result of this program, there would be **savings of millions of dollars a year**. (The New Jersey Institute for Social Justice and the New Jersey Public Policy Research Institute's Re-Entry Roundtable report, June 20, 2003, Trenton, NJ. entitled "Community Re-Entry of Adolescents from N.J.'s Juvenile Justice System," by Bruce B. Stout, Ph.D., University of Medicine and Dentistry of NJ.)

• In the June 28, 2007, *Star Ledger,* an article from Washington, states "Prisons and jails added more than 42,000 inmates last year, the largest increase since 2000.

"Overall, the total number of people behind bars—including those held in local jails—was more than 2.2 million, according to the Justice Department's Bureau of Justice Statistics."

Abby believes that a formalized mentoring program in high schools could reduce these statistics by a quarter, a third, a half, or more. Any significant reduction would be accompanied by a corresponding reduction of costs to taxpayers. That would be a true win-win situation.

She wants teachers to remember, a mentor is someone who has a positive impact on the lives of others, someone who sees more talent, ability, and "specialness" within their mentoree, than the mentoree sees in herself, and someone who helps bring out these special traits and characteristics.

Abby points out that most people have had a mentor at some point in their lives. He or she may have come in the form of a teacher, a parent, a relative, an aunt, uncle, maybe a guardian, an older friend, a counselor, a coach, a minister, priest, rabbi, cleric, tutor, expert – somebody who believed in them, encouraged them to be the best they could be, and someone who had a positive influence on them. Not everyone, however, has been as fortunate, and it is for them that the mentor is here. The mentor now has an opportunity to impact their mentees' lives.

Abby read about actor, Denzel Washington, who believes that his success in life is due to a mentor he had as a teenager in an after-school boys 'club. He was born and raised in a part of New York that was very tough, the streets were tough, gangs were prevalent. He lived in a bad section. And had he taken the wrong path, he certainly would not be the Denzel Washington everyone knows today who is famous and has done such a great job in the movies.

A couple of years ago, he wrote a book called, *A Hand to Guide Me*, which showcases how mentors have shaped the lives of people we all know and respect, from baseball legend Hank Aaron, Mohammed Ali, Bob Woodward – Bob Woodward who was a reporter during the Nixon time. He included people such as Yogi Berra, Danny Glover, the actor, Whoopi Goldberg, and over 60 other famous people. Every one of them had a mentor, somebody who believed in them and encouraged them.

From Greek mythology the riddle that Oedipus answered when he reached the Sphinx is applicable to mentorees. "What walks on four legs in the morning, two legs at noon, and three legs in the evening?" This riddle is associated with man. Four legs relate to crawling as a baby (the morning of our lives), two legs for walking at noon (the middle part of our lives), and three legs in the evening (our twilight years) referring to legs plus a cane. A mentor is similar to a third leg for someone who, at this point in his life, cannot stand alone, even though they are in the middle of their lives.

As Abby frequently stated, "It's amazing how having somebody believe in you really makes you want to do the best that you can do. Sometimes parents or people who are close are just too busy surviving, earning a living; and that's where a mentor comes in. That is exactly what high school mentors will be doing – accepting and encouraging mentees to be the best that he or she can be. Young mentors now have an opportunity to impact their mentee's life."

Being a mentor means showing acceptance and guidance to someone who needs support, i.e., making a difference in someone's life. The reward for the mentor is the tremendous satisfaction awaiting as they watch their mentorees grow and develop into the people they desire to be.

The need for conscientious, sincere, caring, sensitive mentors is overwhelming. If administrators looked at the numbers of kids in trouble, they would have an idea of just how great the need for help is.

"*U.S. News & World Report* reported that, although conventional illiteracy – the inability to read a simple message in any language – had virtually disappeared in the United States, functional illiteracy – the inability to read and write at a level required to function in society – appeared to be increasing" (Myers, *Changing Our Minds, Negotiating English and Literacy*).

These functional illiterates and dropouts started out as unmotivated underachievers, mostly students who didn't fit in and could see no reason to stay in a place where they felt unaccepted and unappreciated, even if those conditions existed only in the student's mind.

Functional illiteracy and school dropouts are major contributors to the escalation of crime in communities, towns, and cities all over the United States.

If mentoring can help lower the number of high school dropouts, it is a program well worth pursuing.

Abby wondered, "Could mentoring reduce these statistics by a quarter, a third a half, or more? Any significant reduction would be accompanied by a corresponding reduction of costs to taxpayers. That would be a true win-win situation."

From Abby's experience, she believes that this program, in action, can prevent many potential dropouts from becoming a negative statistic. How? By simply enabling them to recognize not only their potential but also their positive effect on others.

Success means different things to different people. To Abby it means being of value to yourself, your family, and to society. It means being able to make a difference. It means liking yourself and believing in yourself.

Initially, Abby designed the mentoring programs for the students who needed help, whether academically or socially. To her great surprise, she found that those who benefitted most from the mentoring experience were the mentors.

Statements such as "I felt important," "It was the first time I felt looked up to," "I like the fact that I can be trusted and that I can help someone else," "I know that I need someone to talk to sometimes—being there for someone else is great," "I've learned that I can be a bigger person, a person to go to in a time of trouble," and "I loved helping the underclassmen" were typical of the responses she got on follow-up of the programs.

The responses from parents of those being mentored were also positive. One mother said told Abby that because of his mentor, her son actually looks forward to going to school. Before that, he was scared to leave his home. Teachers commented on improved grades of those being mentored. It's all good!

Abby believes we have to keep in mind one important question: What do gangs have to offer "disaffected" kids? They offer acceptance. She believes we can do better than that. She believes that Kids Mentoring Kids can promote acceptance/validation in a safe environment, in the schools.

How can that be done? Experiencing what it is like to help another person, to make a difference in the life of that person, is more impactful than words could relate. That is what this program is about.

Abby hopes other teachers will join her in the continuous adventure of learning. This is your, the reader's, opportunity to make a difference in the lives of your students.

"One thing I know; the only ones among you who will be really happy are those who will have sought and found how to serve." – Albert Schweitzer

There are kids who are not at risk as well who could use a mentor to help them achieve their goals. This course shows them how.

Kids trained as mentors can have a positive impact on the lives of others. They can see more talent, ability, and "specialness" within their mentoree than those not paying attention can.

This course is designed to help teachers understand the mentoring process-- what a mentor does and how he/she does it. Teachers will learn about the stories of students who have faced daunting challenges in their lives, and they will be introduced to the basic principles of how to best mentor those who are "at risk" for whatever reason.

Mentors will learn how to run a session, the rationale behind mentoring, the Mentor's code of Ethics, Advanced Mentoring Ideas, self esteem/values, and interpersonal skills. Also included are motivational book summaries which give additional invaluable and timeless ideas.

This program was originally designed to help underclassmen adjust to high school, to gain confidence in themselves, and to have someone in the school they could rely on.

As previously stated, the evaluations came as a total surprise. The mentors were more frequently the benefactors. They said things such as, "I loved being a mentor because no one had ever looked up to me before. I felt important. I felt respected." You can't teach those things; you can only experience them. That's why **Kids Mentoring Kids** is so important to have in every school.

This program is self-explanatory and self-taught. In addition to the videos, there are transcripts of the videos, assignment sheets, handouts of all sorts, and materials to supplement every aspect of the course.

Abby had written the book, "The Validating Mentor" with the expectation that adults could mentor students. When she learned that it takes 6 months to clear someone interested in working with students—background check, fingerprinting, etc.—she chose to revise the material and encourage students to be mentors.

The concepts contained in this course work equally as well with friends, family, co-workers, or anyone who desires to improve his life and/or self-concept.

These are some of the kids who need your help. Many are high school dropouts or potential dropouts, young people who must learn to take 100% responsibility for all of their actions and who need your guidance to do so. These are the young adults who desire your help. Nobody gets through life without help. Everyone needs support and validation. Young people need help in every stage of their development.

Many of these "at risk" young adults may honestly wonder if they can change. "Assume a virtue, if you have it not" is the admonition Shakespeare would have given them.

Abby believes that students need to be encouraged to start acting as they desire to be, and they need to know they can be whatever they desire, one step at a time. The capacity for creating the life they want resides within each of them.

Being a mentor means showing acceptance and guidance to someone who needs your support. Your reward is the tremendous satisfaction awaiting you as you watch your mentorees grow and develop into the people they desire to be.

A mentor is a coach who seeks, finds, and points out the strengths of his mentoree. *Validation* implies recognition of someone's strengths.

A mentor is someone who has a positive impact on the lives of others, someone who sees more talent, ability, and "specialness" within their mentoree, than the mentoree sees in herself, and someone who helps bring out these special traits and characteristics.

Abby wants everyone to understand that student mentors are not trained nor are they equipped to deal with medical and/or mental illnesses, alcoholism and/or drug addiction. If a mentor suspects a problem, he/she should notify the appropriate person.

She wants all mentors to understand that any information obtained in connection with mentoring activities is considered confidential. Conversations and observations made regarding the mentoree and/or the mentoree's family will be held in confidence. Exceptions to this confidentiality statement include concerns that the following harm may occur or is currently occurring:

1. Physical, sexual or emotional abuse
2. Suicide
3. Illegal weapons
4. Substance abuse
5. Danger to self and/or others

In the above-mentioned instances, Abby stresses, the mentor is obligated to bring the concerns to the attention of the appropriate authorities or school personnel, if applicable.

As part of the training, Abby wants to make sure the mentor understands that the person being mentored, the mentoree, decides the direction, the speed, the route, the environment, the degree of intensity; and the mentor supports each step she takes.

The student mentor encourages the best direction, the appropriate speed, the best route, the cleanest environment, the safest coworkers, and the appropriate degree of intensity.

By the end of a year's mentoring, hopefully each mentoree will be able to successfully take her place and walk alone without the aid of a mentor.

Abby emphasizes that in order to maximize their potential, *mentorees first must feel they are safe, accepted, and respected as they are.* What helps to instill this feeling is constantly seeing the invisible tattoo on their foreheads, which reads, "Please make me feel important." In other words, "Don't criticize me or make me feel like a loser."

It is a mentor's job to help mentorees move through phase three, *Social-Acceptance* and phase four, *Self-Esteem*, in order to facilitate their reaching the highest level, Five, *Self-Actualization*. This final phase puts the mentoree in a position to make a difference in the world.

Abby emphasizes that feeling important is one of the deepest needs all human beings desire to have fulfilled. The words imply *acceptance*, and they imply *capability*, which is the basis of Level Three on the Hierarchy, *"Belongingness or Social Acceptance." Everyone wants to be accepted,* either by their peers, family, church choir, motorcycle gang, colleagues, or whoever is important to them in their lives.

Once the feelings of acceptance occur, mentorees can reach toward the next Level, *"Esteem/Ego Status."* The Validating Mentor facilitates movement from one level to another, as can be seen in the *Mentoring Code of Ethics*.

Abby states that in one way or another, people young and old will gravitate toward someone who provides a source of validation. Validation is a human need, and this is where being a mentor comes into play. This is their opportunity to help mentorees experience acceptance and validation.

The fifth level of the Hierarchy is *Making a Difference*. With the help of mentors, mentorees will be at the point where they can make a difference--in their own lives and in the lives of those for whom they care.

Abby stressed it is important to remember that *positives do work*. If mentorees believe they can improve, they will. George Reeves, sixth grade teacher of Norman Vincent Peale told his special student, "You can if you think you can." And Peale proved his teacher right.

Overcoming years of negativity and poor results may be the greatest challenge for those who are unmotivated. While mentorees 'improvement may not be vast, their improvement is possible by moving in small increments toward a higher level of proficiency in their job skills and their interpersonal skills.

ENTHUSIASM

Abby reminds mentors of the need to *show lively enthusiasm,* especially with an unmotivated mentoree. If the mentor shows no enthusiasm, the mentoree will reflect none. We "mirror" what we see, and this population is no exception to this rule. And if we don't feel it, again, as previously stated, take Shakespeare's advice, "Assume a virtue, if you have it not." Or, in the vernacular, "Fake it until you make it."

It is human nature to desire fun or pleasure over pain. Mentoring in an atmosphere of fun and/or pleasure enables young people to pay closer attention and retain direction better.

Abby's philosophy behind *The Validating Mentor* consists of five specific provisions:

(1) provides a **safe atmosphere**--physically and mentally (no insults, no making someone wrong, no demeaning comments),

(2) validates students through their efforts by **recognizing what they have done well** or done correctly,

(3) establishes **relevance**--something they can relate to--in their assignments, and

(4) **builds on their successes.** This philosophy of learning also

(5) introduces the element of **fun,** a guaranteed way to encourage learning and growth.

Under the appropriate conditions, validating mentoring can be the foundation for

(1) improved self-esteem and

(2) self-concept, and

(3) improved interpersonal skills.

These benefits are not so surprising if one looks closely at the concepts inherent in the principles of human nature.

Validating mentoring means taking a personal interest in a mentoree, supporting the paths she takes.

Validating mentoring means helping the mentoree strive toward his highest aspirations, not only in career choice but also in the pursuit of happiness in his life.

Validating mentors share their knowledge and experiences in the hope that their mentoree will reach a high level of achievement.

Validating mentors promote the importance of responsibility both at home and away from it.

Validating mentors care about the well-being of themselves and their families and model the behavior they want their mentorees to follow.

Validating mentors receive the greatest gift--satisfaction in knowing they have made a difference.

Charles Engelhardt said it best: "The time to be happy is now. The place to be happy is here, and the way to be happy is by helping others."

WHAT ARE THE CAUSES OF THE PROBLEM?

According to Abby's research the causes of the problem relates to students ' homes and socio-economic backgrounds, parents who are in the "survival" state and do not have adequate time for their children, the attraction of gang membership, the school's lack of effectiveness due to lack of resources, the lack of competence of some teachers are a few of the obvious reasons why students lose interest in school and end up dropping out.

Other students with similar backgrounds, however, frequently overcome these causes; therefore, society has an obligation to look further for remedies to vastly reduce these challenges.

What is the one thing that every human being wants? "Acceptance" by somebody or some group may be a good guess. "Acceptance" can also explain the popularity of gangs, people who accept one another.

A distaste for reading appears to be a universal condition among students who drop out of school and get into trouble with the law. The average reading level of prisoners is at a third-grade level. Unfortunately, their abhorrence of reading causes a domino effect: they don't like to read; therefore, they cannot write well, nor can they do well in other subjects. The result is they drop out. And then what?

A second reason students drop out of school could be boredom, which is intensified by what they consider *irrelevant material,* which in itself is a third cause. Repeated studies have shown that students are more likely to achieve when they are offered materials that are interesting and relevant to their needs (Berliner, *The Manufactured Crisis*).

A fourth cause for dropping out of school could very well be the lack of success that students have encountered throughout their schooling. Lack of success frequently equates to lack of confidence and lack of self-esteem, two major roadblocks to successful learning experiences and, conversely, two motivators for getting into trouble.

When students have experienced continual failure throughout their schooling, by the time they are in high school, their course may seem to be set. Students 'lack of motivation can be attributed partially to the fact that they had not done well in previous classes. As David Berliner argues, "If we foolishly structure schools so that many students are regularly bored, threatened, or punished in them, who would be so naive as to assume those students would thereafter love learning?" (Berliner 349).

Lastly, many of these students do not feel valued by their teachers. Why? One reason is they are on the track, which is perceived by many educators as *inferior*, therefore, the students must be the same.

The "tracked" kids are those who are always in trouble, the kids who don't care, the kids who have been tracked from their elementary years on through high school, in spite of studies which confirm the fact that tracking works to the disadvantage of most children (Berliner 207). Their opinions do not count.

Unfortunately, "students believe that tracking decisions reflect judgments about their personal abilities and prospects; thus, those decisions set up expectations in students that tend to become self-fulfilling prophecies. This means that ability and tracking systems repeatedly give most students the cruel and unfair message that they just don't measure up" (Berliner 322). This message has a definite adverse effect on self-esteem.

WHAT ARE SOME SOLUTIONS?

Many of the primary causes of poor performance in school (dislike of reading, boredom, irrelevance, lack of previous success, and tracking) can be addressed with a revitalized curriculum which enables students to experience success, but that is the responsibility of the local school districts and unfortunately out of the purview of the average citizen.

Mentors can address this need by having students first learn their strengths (we all have some) and aptitudes and then exposing them to the opportunities available to them. Our goal as mentors is to take them out of the "failure" category.

In an attempt to undo the negativity most "dropouts" experienced in school, mentors can encourage (but don't insist on) them to get their high school diplomas either through the country vocational school or their GED through the local colleges. This step, however, is not a requirement for continued mentoring.

Abby's one goal is to help students and young adults prepare themselves to be in the position to obtain well-paying jobs, not minimum wage opportunities. When students do what they enjoy doing, they are apt to be more productive and more successful. Contact with someone who cares is invaluable.

TOP 15 BENEFITS OF WORKING WITH A MENTOR

1. Mentors are familiar with you, your background, your interests, and your goals.
2. Mentors can help you uncover old dreams and activities that made you feel special.
3. Mentors can help you to follow through on your life's purpose.
4. Mentors can help you earn a good living wage.
5. Mentors can help you find greater happiness in your life.
6. Mentors can help you learn how to complete your past.
7. Mentors can help you restore your energy.
8. Mentors can help you get your needs met.
9. Mentors can help you capitalize on your skills and abilities.

10.   Mentors can help you live by your value system.
11.   Mentors can help you eliminate things in your life that are not in your best interests.
12.   Mentors can help you maintain an upbeat, positive attitude.
13.   Mentors can help you handle difficult, challenging situations.
14.   Mentors can help you develop a stronger community.
15.   Mentors can help you be the best person you can be.

The way the mentor knows so much about those they are mentoring is because the mentor will help their mentoree complete the following forms:

• **PERSONAL CHALLENGES**, a one-page list of questions about what the mentoree wants out of life. This is good for the mentor to complete as well.

• **ASSESSMENT**. This is a two-page rating form which will help the mentoree figure out how he/she feels about their environment, personal well-being, mental well-being, relationships, vocation/career/finance areas of their life.

• **10 Goals to Reach in the Next 90 Days**, a page which helps the mentoree set goals for now and for the future.

Two additional pages – **SAMPLE SKILLS** and **CAUSES/ISSUES** will help the mentor and the mentoree zero in on what's important to each.

The Weekly Preparation Form will be used every week to in order for the mentoree to self-monitor his/her progress.

THINGS TO TALK ABOUT
How we feel about ourselves has an influence on how we live our lives and how we interact with others—our peers, teachers, family members, friends.

Rather than directly asking, "How are you feeling about yourself?" you could ask, **"How do you feel about your classes, your classmates, your teachers."** Try to elicit specific instances of why they feel as they do.

For example, if they state that a teacher is picking on them in math class, ask them to tell you more about that. You may find that math is particularly challenging to them, and here is where you can suggest getting extra help or talking to their guidance counselor about help available.

You could ask, **"What do you want to do when you graduate?"** The answer to this question could give you the information you need to better understand how they are viewing their lives.

Attitudes toward their classmates, teachers, friends, and family will usually come through when they talk about their experiences in school. **Remember, your primary goals are 1) to keep them in school and 2) help them recognize what is special about themselves.**

Each student receives a 2-sided "placemat" with everything they need to know in order to be effective mentors. The copies below are condensed to be part of this chapter, but the one the student receives is on heavy-duty paper and printed on both sides. It can be used as a "cheat sheet" initially until they get their bearings dealing with a mentoree.

-----The Mentoring Leadership Training Workshop-----

"It is okay to be me--the best me I can be!"

MISSION: The mission of the Mentoring Leadership Training Workshop is to train students with the capability for ethical leadership and self-actualization both independently and as members of a community.

GOAL: The goal of The Mentoring Leadership Training Workshop is to provide middle school students with the tools necessary to participate to their fullest in and outside of the school community.

MAJOR BENEFITS FOR THE SCHOOL: Reduced incidents of bullying, improved individual self concepts, and higher graduation rates.

INDIVIDUAL BENEFITS: Enhanced self concept, acceptance, validation, self-actualization.

AMBIANCE FOR ALL MEETINGS

S - A - V - E

S - SAFE

A - ACCEPTANCE

V - VALIDATION

E - ENTHUSIASM

THE MENTORING CODE OF ETHICS
THE BAKER'S DOZEN

General Guidelines for Working With Mentees

1. **SHOW RESPECT TO GET RESPECT**

    Know that your friends "mirror" you. They reflect what they see, hear, and feel from you.

2. **BE NONJUDGMENTAL**

    Accept your classmates as they are, and then provide the atmosphere for them to grow in a positive manner.

3. **SEEK THE STRENGTHS OF YOUR CLASSMATES**

    - Help your peers to recognize their specialness.
    - Remember **that everyone desperately wants to feel special.**
    - See the invisible tattoo on every student's forehead that reads: **"PLEASE MAKE ME FEEL IMPORTANT."**

4. **PROVIDE A SAFE ATMOSPHERE**

5. **KNOW, YOU cannot NOT COMMUNICATE**

6. **SET HIGH EXPECTATIONS**

    Remember the story of a new teacher who thought the locker list from140-160 was the list of IQ's in her class and she treated them accordingly, and they performed accordingly.

7. **MAKE SINCERITY YOUR NUMBER ONE PRIORITY**

8. **BE SENSITIVE**

9. **SET BOUNDARIES**

10. **HAVE FUN!**

11. **SMILE: It warms a room.**

12. **BE (OR ACT) ENTHUSIASTIC** about everything you do. It's contagious.

13. **Remember, PEOPLE HAVE TWO BASIC NEEDS:**
    1) TO KNOW THAT THEY ARE LOVABLE and 2) THAT THEY ARE WORTHWHILE.

Primary Goal of Mentoring Leadership Workshop:
To achieve each student's highest ethical leadership potential according to his or her aptitudes and dreams.

· **Your beliefs guide you.** "If you think you can or you think you can't, you are right." -Henry Ford. Remember the flea and the elephant.

Confidentiality EXCEPT if you become aware of

- Physical, sexual, or emotional abuse
- Suicide possibility
- Illegal weapons
- Substance Abuse
- Danger to self or others

QUESTIONING
- **Ask question**
- **Paraphrase**
- **Pause**
- **Question**

Listening
- Be silent
- Hear words spoken and not spoken
- Listen with senses
- Reflect back what you hear
- Ask for further clarification
- Prompts

Listen for
- Authenticity and Truth (tone & language)
- True desires
- Fears
- Support
- Positives
- Your reactions to mentee

Non-Verbal Communication
You Cannot NOT Communicate

55% - What you SEE
38% - What you HEAR
7% - Words used

Preparation Form
- What accomplished since last session?
- What didn't get done, but intended to?
- Challenges and problems?
- Opportunities available now?
- What I want to work on today?
- What I promise to do by next meeting.

Dale Carnegie's Human Relation Skills
- Do not criticize, condemn or complain
- Give honest, sincere appreciation
- Arouse in other person an eager want
- Become genuinely interested in others
- Smile - it warms a room
- A person's name is the sweetest sound
- Be a good listener
- Talk in terms of other people's interest
- Make the person feel important

Things to Talk About
- How are you feeling about yourself?
- How are you looking at your life?
- How are you feeling about others?
- What has occurred since our last meeting?
- Any breakthroughs or insights?
- New choices or decisions made?
- Personal news?

More Talking Points
- Progress on goals, projects, activities?
- What have you done that you're proud of?
- What resistance are you encountering?
- Can I explain something for you?
- Can I provide you with more information?
- Do you need help developing a plan?
- May I offer you a strategy or advice?
- What is your next goal or project?

"Wants"
- Where do you want to live, work, school?
- How do you want to look, feel, sound?
- What do you want to do every day?
- Desired relationships with family, friends?
- What obstacles do you see keeping you from doing what you want in life?
- How can I help you succeed?

Interests
- What do you feel strongly about? News that upsets you on TV?
- Whom do you admire and why?
- Where do you enjoy being?
- What do you do in your spare time?

CHAPTER SEVEN
Recommended Action

Abby knows that teacher training is constantly changing and evolving. She also believes we live in stressful times, times that may make us question our own values, question our own worth. That's why outside validation is so vitally important. These three courses provide that validation and are well worth the time to learn and use in your own classroom.

As a reminder of the testimonials Abby's Speaking for Teens class has received, check them out. The entire 19 pages can be found at https://bit.ly/2Mkflgc.

Another option is to visit https://www.cassidycourses.com and learn about the three programs already fully developed. A brief video precedes each lesson explaining what should be covered. Each lesson also contains slides for every class, downloadable information for the students, and a script for the session. All of the work has been done in order to facilitate the training.

Either way, Abby would be delighted if you shared in her belief that a strong self-concept is essential to the success of any person. "What the mind can conceive and believe, it can achieve." -Napoleon Hill; but first a person has to believe in him- or herself.

Abby believes that every child can experience a high level of self-esteem, which, of course, leads to self-actualization, the top of Maslow's Hierarchy of Needs.

Abby believes that people, especially kids, can live their own framework of beliefs, guiding principles when they believe in themselves. They can then ask: What is my personal role in the world?

Helen Keller said, "The only thing worse than being blind is having sight but no vision." These courses provide the vision, the self-belief, and the confidence to pursue their goals.

Henry Thoreau said, "Go confidently in the direction of your dreams. Live the life you have imagined." This, of course, is possible if a person believes in himself and his or her ability to do so.

As you believe, so you are.